D0708470

all colour book of
Insects

by Michael Tweedie

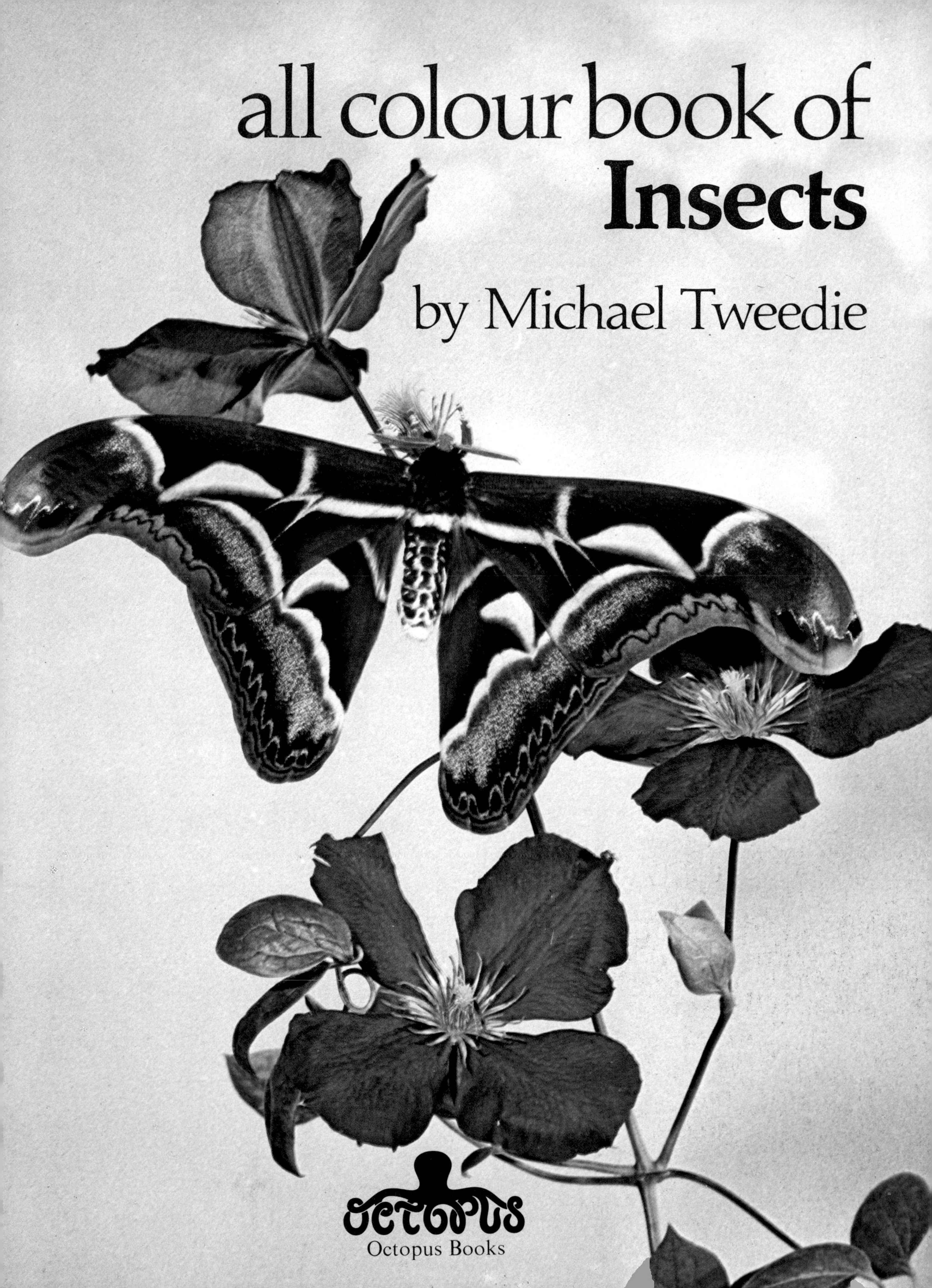

Octopus Books

First published in 1973 by
Octopus Books Limited,
59 Grosvenor Street, London W1

ISBN 0 7064 0218 9

Produced by Mandarin Publishers Limited,
77a Marble Road, North Point, Hong Kong
Printed in Hong Kong

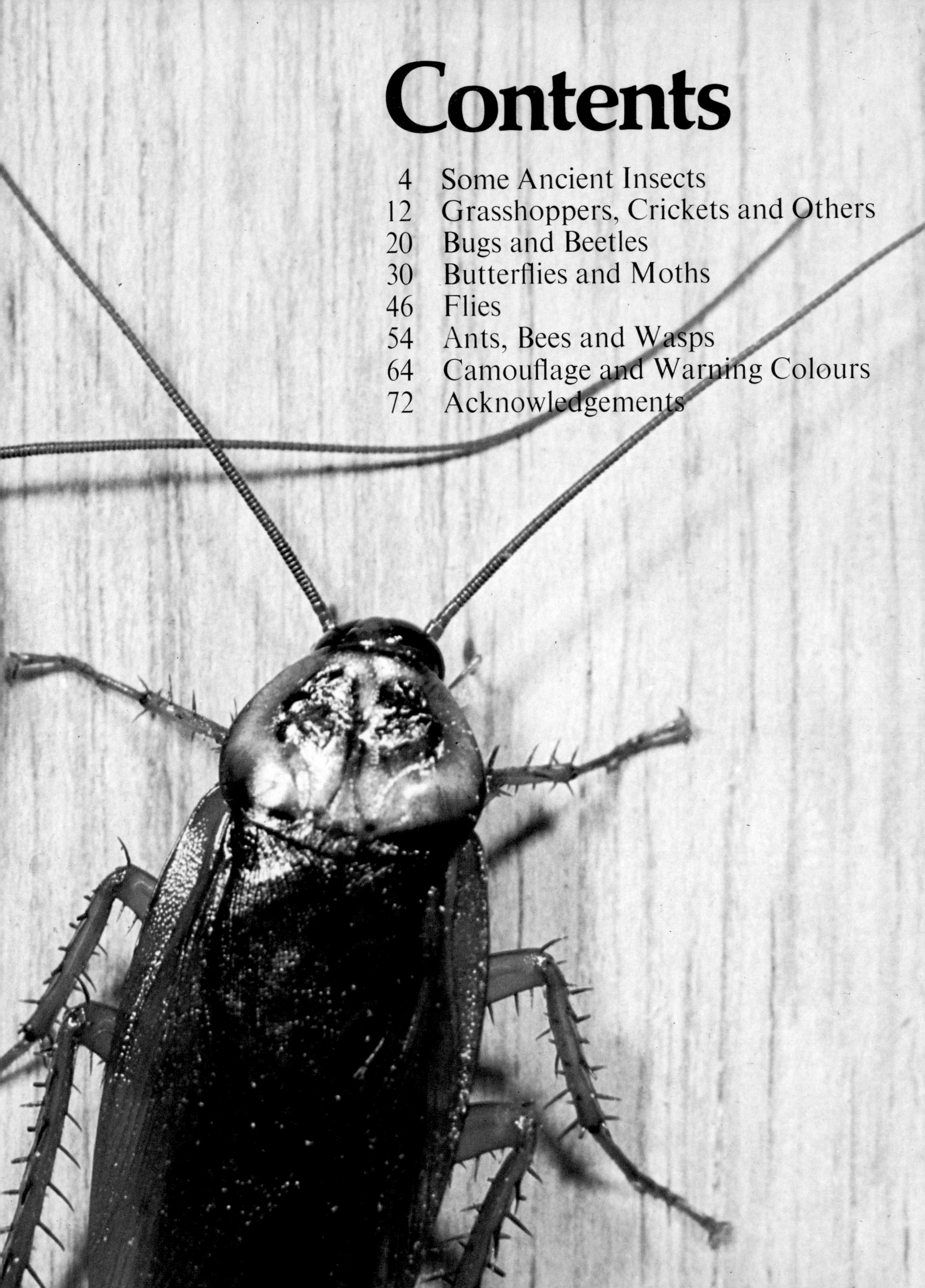

Contents

Some Ancient Insects

The fossil record informs us that the sea became populated with living creatures long before the land, which remained, for millions of years, a lifeless desert. Some four or five hundred million years ago plants became adapted to live first on the sea shore and later in swampy places on the land itself. Then came the first land animals, which included arachnids, that is relatives of the scorpions and spiders, and the earliest insects.

These are represented by fossils in a flint-like rock found at Rhynie in Scotland, which also contains beautifully preserved remains of primitive rush-like land plants. The age of these fossils is between 350 and 400 million years, the so-called Devonian period. The insects are not, as might be expected, of a totally unfamiliar type, but are springtails or *Collembola*, an order of insects found today in abundance in a great variety of situations. They are most plentiful in the soil of pasture and woodland, where quite astonishing population figures have been estimated, 200 to 300 millions to the acre. They live in snowfields on high mountains and also farther south in the Antarctic than any other insects, except a few parasites of birds. One species is a pest in fields of lucerne or alfalfa, another in artificial mushroom beds. A few, including the one illustrated, are found in countless numbers on the surface film of water in weedy ponds and ditches. The springtails, though primitive, are not regarded as the ancestors of modern insects, and there is even some doubt whether they should be classified with the insects at all. Their most characteristic feature is a forked organ, attached to the tail and folded forwards under the body. By flicking this downwards a springtail can jump into the air like a flea. None of them ever has wings.

The *Thysanura* or bristle-tails are also primitively wingless. By this we mean that they have been so all through their evolutionary history; there are many 'higher' insects that are wingless but close study of them provides evidence that they have descended from winged ancestors. On the other hand the bristle-tails are undoubtedly true insects, primitive survivors of an ancestral type that existed before any insects had developed wings. The most familiar of them is the little Silverfish (*Lepisma saccharina*) that lives in kitchen cupboards all over the world. This is a 'domesticated' insect, entirely unknown in the wild state, and it has lived in this way certainly for over 2,000 years, for it is recognizably described in a Chinese dictionary compiled between the fourth and second centuries BC. Bristle-tails are delicate little creatures, very rarely preserved as fossils, and they must have existed far earlier than the Triassic period from which come their earliest fossil remains so far discovered.

Another group of very primitive insects of which a number of species have become 'domesticated' are the cockroaches. They are not very numerous in the wild state and would be highly regarded as 'living fossils' if some of them had not become such unwelcome invaders of our homes. Cockroaches similar to those living today inhabited the swampy forests of the Carboniferous period whose remains provide the substance of most of the world's coalfields. This gives the cockroaches a respectable pedigree of at least 300 million years, and they were among the earliest animals ever to fly in the air.

The fine network of supporting veins in the wings of dragonflies and damselflies (order *Odonata*) is regarded as a primitive characteristic, and they too are an ancient group of insects. The true dragonflies were abundant during the time of the dinosaurs, and first appeared some millions of years before the giant reptiles came on the scene. The dinosaurs flourished from about 200 million to 65 million years ago. The largest insects of which we have any knowledge were close relatives and probably ancestors of the dragonflies. They lived in the great swampy forests of the Carboniferous period, together with the early cockroaches, and their wings had a span of up to 27 inches. They are the only fossil insects of dramatically large size.

Dragonflies and damselflies pass their early stages in the water and are hunters of other insects and small animals throughout their lives. The nymphs or larvae of the larger species can do serious damage in fish hatcheries.

May-flies (order *Ephemeroptera*) share with the dragonflies the character of a primitive net-like wing venation. They have a long life as aquatic larvae, sometimes several years, and a very short existence as winged adults, a few hours or at most a few days. The adults take no food, but inflate their stomachs with air to give their bodies extra buoyancy in flight. They are wholly unique among the insects in the fact that they shed their skins once again after the wings are fully developed.

All insects grow by a series of stages, called instars, moulting their skins at the beginning of each instar and growing rapidly after each moult or ecdysis. In the more primitive types of insects, including cockroaches, dragonflies and may-flies, there is little change in the bodily form during growth, apart from increase in size and gradual development of the wings. Such insects are said to be hemimetabolous or to have incomplete metamorphosis. Insects like butterflies, in which development involves profound changes in form, from larva to pupa and from pupa to perfect insect or imago, have complete metamorphosis and are called holometabolous.

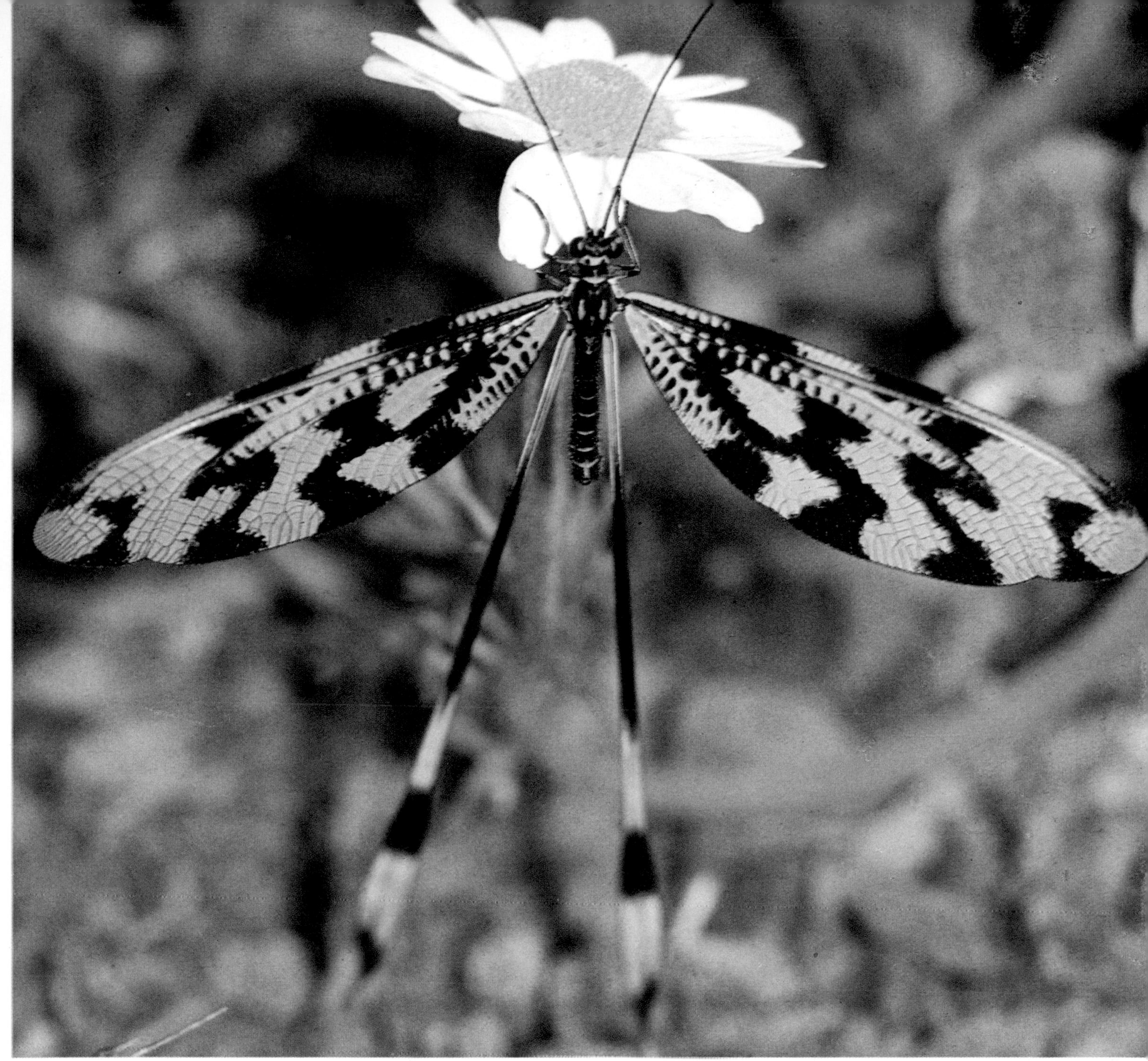

The hemimetabolous condition is, of course, the more primitive (though less so than that of wingless insects like the silverfish, which grow without any metamorphosis), but some of the insects with larva and pupa stages date from early geological times. The most varied of these, the *Neuroptera* or nerve-winged insects, range back in time to the Permian period, 250 million years ago, long before dinosaur time. The lacewings are the most familiar members of this order, delicate insects with soft bodies and gauzy wings. Their larvae, however, are predators and lead useful lives hunting and devouring aphids or greenfly. Some species have the strange habit of first sucking out the internal juices of their prey and then piling the empty skins on their backs, entangling them among the bristles that grow there. A large type of lacewing with aquatic larvae is common in North America, where they are called Dobson flies.

The most beautiful of the lacewings are the *Nemopteridae* or thread-winged lacewings. They have patterned wings, and on the hind-wings long thread-like or ribbon-like tails. They are found where rather hot, dry climates prevail, from southern Europe and Africa eastward to Australia.

Scorpion-flies (*Mecoptera*) are so called because the external genital organs of the males have the form of a forward-curving capsule, rather like a scorpion's sting. Not many species are known, but some of them are common in temperate regions, especially in woods, where they can be recognized by the distinct dark pattern on the wings. They date back to the same period as the nerve-winged insects, and are regarded as living representatives of the common ancestor of the flies, butterflies and moths and some other orders of insects.

It is difficult to imagine the remoteness in time of the geological periods we have mentioned. If time is represented on a scale of a yard to a thousand years, that of Christ would be just six feet away. On this scale the Devonian period, when the earliest known springtails lived, would be rather over 200 MILES away.

Previous page: left:
May-fly *(Ephemera).* May-flies are of great interest to fly fishermen because they appear in swarms over water and stimulate trout to feed so eagerly that they are readily taken with artificial lures. The early stages of may-flies are passed in water. When fully grown they come to the surface, cast off the larval skin and, having expanded their wings, fly away and settle on a rush or reed, where the skin is cast again. Fishermen call the may-flies of the first winged stage 'duns'. The species of the genus *Ephemera* are the largest of the British may-flies.

Previous page: right:
Thread-winged Lacewing *(Nemoptera sinuata).* This family of lacewings includes the most beautiful of all the order *Nemoptera.* They take their name from the long, narrow prolongation on each hind-wing, rather like that of a swallow tail butterfly. The larvae are most peculiar creatures with flat heads and slender 'necks' which are sometimes as long as the rest of the body. They live in sand and prey on small insects. The specimen shown here was photographed in Turkey.

Below:
Water Springtail *(Podura aquatica).* This tiny insect is common on water at the edges of ditches and ponds where there is a good growth of water plants. They live on the surface film and when abundant look like specks of soot, crawling and jumping about. They jump by means of a forked organ on the underside of the body. Although they do not go under the water, they will soon die if removed to a dry container due to loss of body water by evaporation. The picture shows the springtails in various stages of growth, the bluish-black adults, pink juveniles and individuals of intermediate size and colour. White cast skins can also be seen.

Bottom:
Silverfish *(Lepisma saccharina).* Inhabitants of houses over a great part of the world, Silverfish live in kitchens and larders and also in places where books and papers are stored. They probably do more harm in the latter habitat as they like all kinds of gum and size, including the emulsion of photographs. They are not known to live anywhere in the wild state. Silverfish hide away during the day but you can often see them when a light is switched on after some hours of darkness, and they are sometimes trapped in slippery basins and baths.

Right:
American Cockroach *(Periplaneta americana).* This is the largest of the so-called domesticated cockroaches that live in human dwellings, and is the dominant species in tropical countries. Its name was bestowed on it by an eighteenth-century zoologist who believed mistakenly that it was a native of America. Its original home is most probably North Africa and it has been carried all over the world by ships. This and several other kinds of cockroach are among the most unpleasant of all indoor insect pests. The amount of stored food they eat is not very important, but they foul and render inedible far more than they consume.

Below:
Southern Aeshna Dragonfly *(Aeshna cyanea).* All dragonflies pass their early stages in water and the females of the different species lay their eggs in different ways to ensure that they will hatch in a suitable environment. The big Hawker Dragonflies of the genus *Aeshna* insert their eggs into the stems of water plants or in debris beside or floating on the water. This one is laying in damp moss beside a pond. Other kinds of dragonflies lay their eggs by skimming the surface and dipping the tip of their abdomen in the water; the eggs then sink to the bottom.

Right:
Dragonfly *(Orthetrum farinosum).* Dragonflies are found everywhere except in the coldest regions of the world. Collecting them is not very rewarding because the beautiful colours of their bodies are difficult to preserve. They are splendid subjects for photography and, as they are large and fly by day, their habits can easily be observed and recorded. One can work in the same way as bird watchers do, with field-glasses and a note book, and there is still a great deal to be learnt about dragonflies in tropical countries in particular. This beautiful species is a native of South Africa.

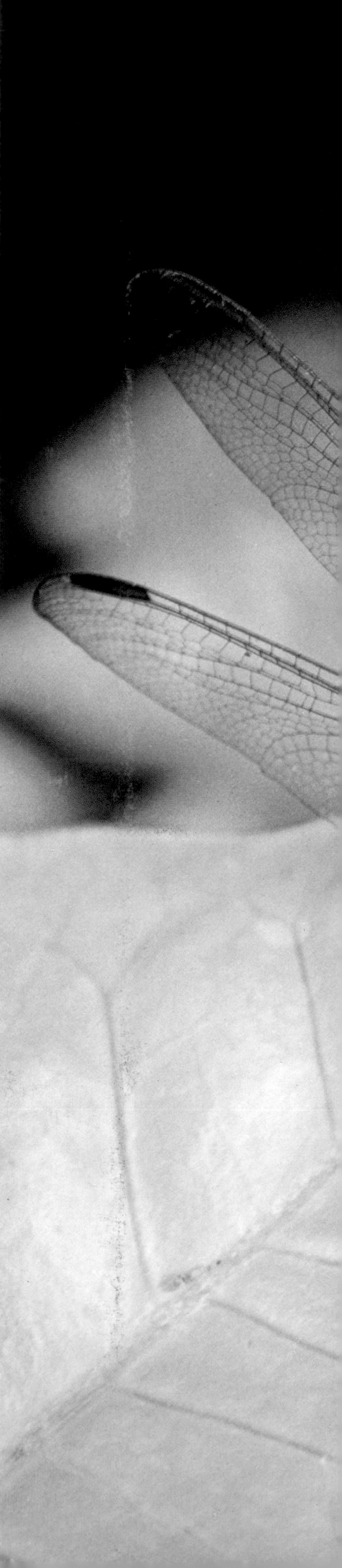

Left:
Scorpion-fly *(Panorpa communis).* The light and dark chequered wings make scorpion-flies easy to recognize. Although they are perfectly harmless the males appear to have a sting like that of a scorpion; this is really the external genital apparatus. Females lack this feature but are otherwise similar to the males. The front part of the head in both sexes is elongated to form a conspicuous downward-pointing beak, at the tip of which are the biting mouth-parts. The larvae burrow in the soil and both adults and larvae feed mainly on dead insects. This species is common in woodland in Britain and Europe.

Below:
Green Lacewing *(Chrysopa).* The green lacewings, of which several species are common in Britain and Europe, are delicate insects with gauzy wings and bright golden eyes. They are common in woods and along hedgerows and lay their eggs on leaves. The eggs are curious, each one being raised on a fine, hair-like stalk. The larvae are voracious eaters of aphids. One species of green lacewing, *Chrysopa carnea*, hibernates through the winter, often in houses. During hibernation it loses its green colour and turns dull brown.

Right:
Dobson-fly *(Corydalis).* The Dobson-flies are related to the Alder-flies, both groups having aquatic larvae and being found generally near water. The genus *Corydalis* is found in Asia and North America and some of them are large with a wing span of nearly six inches. The males have

11

very long, sickle-like mandibles; this one is a female. The big larvae of Dobson-flies are called hellgrammites in America and fishermen value them highly as bait.

Below:
Common Coenagria *(Coenagria puella).* This is one of the damselflies, which are included in the same order as the dragonflies and have similar habits. Damselflies are always slender with weak fluttering flight, very unlike the swift, powerful flight of dragonflies. Also they rest with their wings raised over their backs, not extended on each side like dragonflies. Damselflies have the body variously coloured, often very delicate and beautiful; the wings are usually clear, but are coloured and patterned in some species.

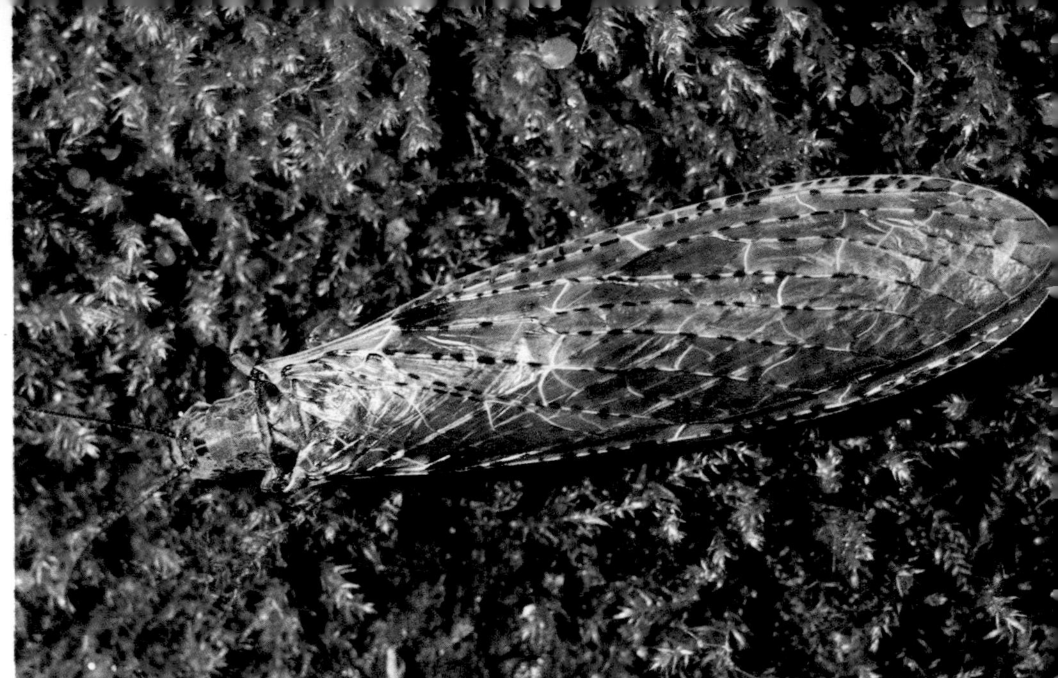

Grasshoppers, Crickets and Others

In a sense this chapter is a continuation of the last because all the insects included in it are of the more primitive type, having incomplete metamorphosis. That is to say the development of the wings is the only important change in form during the course of their growth. We will say no more about their geological history except to mention that the *Orthoptera* (grasshoppers and crickets) are almost as ancient as the cockroaches.

Most of the *Orthoptera* have the hind pair of legs greatly enlarged for the purpose of powerful jumping, and this characteristic makes them easy to identify. Another feature common to most of them is the ability to make sounds by which members of the same species communicate and conduct their courtship. The sounds are always produced by the method of stridulation, when a hard ridge is stroked over a number of closely set projections; stroking your finger nail along the teeth of a comb provides an illustration of it.

They fall into two well marked groups, the grasshoppers and locusts on the one hand and the crickets and bush-crickets on the other. The former have short antennae, stridulate by rubbing the hind-leg against a ridge on the wing and have their hearing organs at the base of the abdomen. The crickets and bush-crickets have long, thread-like antennae, stridulate by rubbing one wing over the other and have their ears, in the form of minute pits, on the tibiae or wrists of the fore-limbs.

Locusts are simply large grasshoppers, and the term is best confined to those species which sometimes appear in huge swarms and completely destroy the vegetation over many square miles of country. These are found mostly in tropical and subtropical regions, and the swarming is always the result of a localized build-up of numbers. The crowding that results stimulates the insects to greater activity and further urge to crowd together and then finally to migrate. At first they are flightless and known as 'hoppers', later when they are mature they continue to migrate by air, flying great distances and descending at intervals to feed and breed, so that the swarm continues to build up its numbers. The aggregate weight of locusts in a large swarm has been estimated at about 15,000 tons. There are several species of plague locusts; the most widespread is the Migratory Locust (*Locusta migratoria*), but the Desert Locust (*Schistocerca gregaria*) of northern Africa and western Asia is the most damaging and difficult to control.

The smaller grasshoppers are harmless and attractive creatures and the chirping of the males is a welcome sound in meadows. Each species has an individual song which can be recognized, just as bird songs can.

The crickets include the House Cricket (*Acheta domestica*) and the Field Crickets (genus *Gryllus*), both famed for their cheerful singing. House crickets were at one time dwellers in houses in many parts of the world, just as cockroaches are, but are far less dirty and unpleasant, in fact they were often regarded as welcome. The modern obsession with hygiene has almost banished them from our homes but they have learned to live in the huge municipal rubbish dumps, taking advantage of the warmth from burning and decay. They live naturally in the open in North Africa and western Asia. The field crickets, of which a number of species are found in Europe, North America and temperate Asia, are sometimes kept as pets in little cages in southern Europe, Japan and no doubt in other regions as well, for the sake of their cheerful singing. It is also entertaining to put two males together, for they will usually fight, chirping vigorously as they do so, and they seldom hurt each other.

Crickets are ground dwellers. Their relatives among the trees and bushes are the bush-crickets, which are often green in colour and slender with very long legs. They are as vocal as the rest of the *Orthoptera* but, unlike grasshoppers, most of them sing at night. Some of them are called Katydids in America because their song suggests this combination of syllables.

The Mole Crickets are perhaps the strangest of all this group of insects. As their name suggests they are burrowers and their fore-legs are adapted for digging in very much the same way as the front limbs of a mole. The hind-legs are short and not modified for jumping. Mole crickets have a loud sustained song which starts just as the sun goes down.

The Stick-insects and Leaf-insects (*Phasmida*) are a mainly tropical group, mostly large and rather sluggish. Many of them furnish outstanding examples of natural camouflage. Stick-insects depend on their extremely attenuated shape to achieve a resemblance to stems and twigs, and some of them rest in attitudes which assist the illusion. The leaf-insects display remarkably exact and detailed simulation of leaves. One Indian species of stick-insect, *Carausius morosus*, is often kept in captivity both for amusement and experiment, and is known as the Laboratory Stick-insect. Its reproduction is peculiar in that it does not require fertilization of the female by a male. Males are in fact extremely rare and occur in a proportion of one to many hundreds of females. This type of reproduction is known as parthenogenesis.

There is little in the appearance of praying mantises to suggest their close relationship with cockroaches, but the two groups are included in one order, the

Dictyoptera. Similarities are apparent in the arrangement of the veins of the wings and also in the mode of egg laying. All mantises are predatory and have the fore-legs specially adapted for seizing prey. The two largest segments, the femur and tibia, are spined and fold against each other rather like the blade and handle of a pen knife. Mantises do not pursue their victims but lie in wait for them. Some of them can be remarkably well camouflaged, disguising themselves as green or brown leaves or even as flowers.

Termites form an order of insects of their own, the *Isoptera*; here again cockroaches come into the picture, for they are undoubtedly the termites' nearest relatives. On the other hand termites are not remotely related to the ants, which they resemble so closely that people often call them 'white ants'. The resemblance arises from the fact that ants and termites have arrived, through convergent evolution, at a very similar mode of life. Both are social insects living in enormously populous colonies of which the great majority are non-reproductive forms called workers. One fundamental difference between termites and ants is that the workers in a termite colony are a mixture of sterile males and females; all ant workers are females. The male ant dies after mating and the reproductive female or queen never meets a male again; among termites a fertile king and queen, often called the royal pair, live together. Finally, termites have incomplete metamorphosis, starting life as miniature replicas of the adults, while ants go through larva and pupa stages.

The nests of some kinds of termites are enormous structures towering nearly 20 feet high, and made of an extremely hard composition of earth and the termites' saliva or excrement. Some kinds feed on wood, and although their natural food is fallen trees in forests, they cannot distinguish between this and structural timber and do immense damage to wooden buildings in tropical countries.

Earwigs are curious little insects which would be quite obscure if one or two species were not very abundant. Everyone knows the common earwig, *Forficula auricularia*; gardeners hate them in spite of the fact that they kill a great many small caterpillars. Nearly all of them are small, but a relatively gigantic earwig, three to four inches long, exists on the island of St Helena.

Previous page: left:
Common Green Grasshopper *(Omocestus viridulus).* This is a very common species all over Europe and much of temperate Asia, and in the British Isles it extends to Ireland and the north of Scotland. It is variously coloured with either green or brown predominating, and one variety is purple on the sides. The wings are well developed, but few of the small grasshoppers ever fly far, in which they differ from their larger relatives the locusts. The songs of male grasshoppers often indicate their species better than their appearance. That of the Common Green is a loud ticking noise, each burst of song usually lasting from 10 to 20 seconds.

Previous page: right:
Brown Locust *(Locusta pardalina).* This species is the endemic plague locust of southern Africa. The picture shows young locusts or 'hoppers' congregating together in the early stages of the formation of a swarm. If unchecked they will continue to build up their numbers until they can fly and will then take to the air, still keeping together, and may travel great distances. In South Africa swarms of the Brown Locust originate in the arid Karroo area, where they are now controlled and prevented from swarming in such vast numbers that they become dangerous.

Top left:
Speckled Bush-cricket *(Leptophyes punctatissima).* Bush-crickets are relatives of the true crickets, most of which live in burrows in the ground. The majority of bush-crickets spend their lives among foliage and are green in colour. They differ from grasshoppers (and resemble crickets) in having long, thread-like antennae. This species has exceptionally long hind-legs and is almost wingless, the wings being reduced to small overlapping lobes in the male, which are even smaller in the female. The one shown here is a male. It is common in Britain and Europe generally.

Left:
Dark Bush-cricket *(Pholidoptera griseoaptera).* This species lives among nettles, brambles and other vegetation growing close to the ground, and is always brown in colour, sometimes almost black. The specimen shown is a female and the long, blade-like ovipositor can be clearly seen. She uses it to cut slits in bark or rotten wood, in which to lay her eggs. This is a flightless insect, the wings being very small in the male and reduced to vestiges in the female. A common species in Britain and Europe.

Right:
Mole-cricket *(Gryllotalpa hexadactyla).* The mole-crickets are extraordinary insects, found in most warm and temperate regions of the world. They are highly modified for burrowing; their fore-limbs are stout and spined and turned outwards very much like the front legs of a mole. The body is covered with fine, velvety hair. Most of the species can fly, using the well-developed hind-wings. The male sings with a sustained churring note which he utters at dusk and in the night, sitting at the mouth of his burrow This is a North American species.

Below:
Northern Bush Katydid *(Scudderia septentrionalis).* The bush katydids of North America have narrower wings than the true katydids (*Pterophylla*); both are, in fact, bush-crickets. The name 'Katydid' is a syllabic rendering of the song, which they produce by moving one wing over the other and causing a ridge to scrape over a series of closely-set teeth like those of a comb. The one shown here is a female in the act of using her ovipositor to cut a slit in a leaf, in which she will lay her eggs. Both young and adult feed throughout their lives among the foliage of trees and bushes.

Right:
Bush Grasshoppers *(Phymateus leprosus).* The African grasshoppers of this genus protect themselves from their natural enemies by exuding an acrid-tasting froth from openings near the bases of the legs. When they are young, in the 'hopper' stage, they crowd together in swarms or bands, which may travel many miles. The swarm is surrounded by an aura of the smell of their repugnant fluid, and their warning pattern of stripes is made more conspicuous by their being closely crowded.

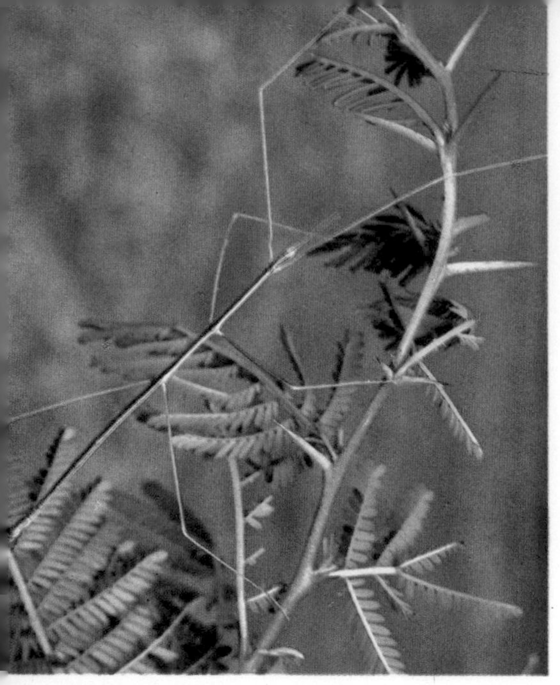

Left:
Stick-insect. The stick-insects and leaf-insects (order *Phasmida*) are almost confined to the tropics and subtropics, and occur all round the world in these latitudes. Most of them are fairly large, some being among the largest of all insects. They always live and feed among vegetation, and are protected by their resemblance to their surroundings; thus their name. Some stick-insects, like this South African species, are extraordinarily attenuated and very difficult to see when they are resting among twigs and branches.

Below:
Earwig *(Forficula auricularia).* Earwigs are not general favourites, but they lead more orderly lives than most insects. A male and female pair in the late summer and hibernate together in a cell in the soil or hollowed out under a stone. Early in the spring the female lays a batch of white eggs, as shown in the picture, and at this time the male leaves her. She remains with the eggs, brooding them and constantly cleaning them with her mouth, and after they hatch she protects the young until they leave the cell. If removed from the mother the eggs invariably become infected with fungus and fail to hatch.

Bottom:
Termites *(Macrotermes bellicosus).* This is a widely distributed African termite that builds large nests above ground. The picture shows a hole that has been broken in the wall of the nest and two of its inhabitants, a worker and a soldier. These are both non-reproductive offspring of the enormously prolific queen, who lives inside the nest. The worker is concerned

with mending the breach, the soldier with guarding it against intruders. It has powerful jaws, capable of drawing blood from a human finger, and the name 'bellicosus', meaning 'warlike', well suits these big-headed warriors.

Right:
Praying Mantis. This African mantis is shown stalking a small moth on a flower. In the second picture it is engaged in eating it, holding it in its formidable, spined fore-limbs, which are specially adapted for seizing and holding prey. Mantises ambush their victims, waiting for insects to settle nearby or actually within reach, and most of them are coloured to match their background of green or withered leaves. This conceals the mantis alike from its intended victims and also from its own enemies, the birds and lizards.

Bugs and Beetles

For most people the word 'bug' means any sort of insect, but entomologists use it to denote an order, the *Hemiptera*, some of which look rather like beetles. It is for this reason that we have chosen to illustrate these two orders together, although they are not at all closely related.

The bugs are the most diverse and successful of the hemimetabolous insects – those that gradually develop wings as they grow but do not change greatly in form. They all have one important characteristic in common; the mouth-parts are modified for piercing and sucking and are in the shape of a beak projecting from the front of the head. Most of them live on the sap of plants, but a large number prey on other insects and a few suck the blood of bigger animals. The subdivision that look like beetles, known as the *Heteroptera*, have the fore-wings divided into horny and membranous areas, and they form a protective covering over the delicate hind-wings, which are folded beneath them. These include the Shield Bugs, many of which are brightly or even luridly coloured, a warning to birds that they are inedible. This is quite apparent if one handles one of these bugs, as they have a strong and disgusting smell. Some of the *Heteroptera* are wingless, and among these is the loathsome bed-bug, which is one of the blood-suckers. Its nearest relatives are all parasites on bats, and it is almost certain that man acquired the bed-bug as a parasite during the Stone Age, when he shared his cave with the bats. A number of the *Heteroptera* are aquatic, some skating on the surface of ponds and streams, while others live actually under water.

The other group of bugs, the sub-order *Homoptera*, have the same sort of sucking beak and feed on plant sap, but they have two pairs of usually transparent gauzy wings which makes them look more like flies than beetles, and many have English names in accordance with this. Aphids or green-fly are the most familiar of them, and are abundant on all sorts of vegetation all over the world. Both by consuming huge quantities of sap and by carrying virus diseases they damage the plants they feed on and are hated by gardeners and farmers alike. In consequence any other insect that preys on aphids is accounted a friend of man. Cicadas are also homopterous bugs and, like the *Orthoptera*, are extremely vocal; their voices are, in fact far louder than those of any other insects. They do not sing by stridulating, but by the rapid vibration of a pair of stiff membranes contained in pockets in the body. Their early stages are passed underground, sucking the sap of roots, and some of them exist in this way as larvae or nymphs for very long periods. Many *Homoptera* are wingless, and among aphids there are usually winged and wingless individuals.

As insects are to other animals in point of numbers of species, so are beetles to other insects. They are by far the largest order with about 275,000 species described and named and several hundred more discovered every year. They range in size from the bulkiest of all insects, the African Goliath beetle to species so minute that their bulk is one eight-millionth of that of the Goliath. They are found in every sort of habitat that will support life, and are most numerous in forests and fertile grasslands, but are also found high on mountains, deep in caves and in the dryest and harshest deserts.

Most beetles have a hard carapace formed by modification of the fore-wings, each of which has the form of a rigid curved shield called an elytron. The two elytra meet each other along the middle line of the back. The head, thorax and under surface of the body also have a hard covering so that the beetle is effectively armoured all over, and also well protected against losing water in very dry conditions. This beautifully jointed coat of mail may well be the feature that has made beetles such successful animals. Many of them can fly by means of the hind-wings, which are large and delicate and, when not in use, lie folded underneath the elytra. These are raised and held out on each side in flight.

Although they are advanced insects with complete metamorphosis, the beetles have retained the primitive chewing mouth-parts characteristic of dragonflies, cockroaches and grasshoppers. Their feeding habits are as varied as their appearance. Many are predators, hunting other insects and especially soft-bodied larvae. The Tiger beetles are perhaps the most efficient of these, and the Ground beetles of the family *Carabidae*, which number more than 24,000 known species, are almost all hunters and killers. The small pretty Ladybird beetles nearly all prey, both as larvae and adults, on aphids, scale insects and other destroyers of plants, and are thus some of the most useful of all insects to man.

In every sort of dead and decaying matter will be found scavenging beetles that specialize in using it as food for themselves and their larvae. A dead bird or rat is quickly discovered by the insects known as Carrion beetles or Sexton beetles. These remarkable creatures, working in pairs, will quickly bury a small animal, shovelling away the earth from beneath it with their specially adapted legs and flattened heads. Once buried the corpse is used as food by the beetles and the female lays her eggs on it so that it provides food for her offspring as well. Many kinds of beetles treat dung in much the same way. These are the well-known scarabs; some of them simply make a burrow and stuff it with dung which they

find on the surface, others shape the dung into balls which they roll away to a situation better suited for burying it than the place where they discovered it. All these beetles do valuable service by keeping the surface of the earth clean and by returning to the soil the large amount of dung which they leave uneaten.

Dead wood is also eaten by some kinds of beetles. In the natural state they are doing a useful service, but, like the termites, they make no distinction between the trunk of a fallen tree and the timbers of a cathedral. The Death-watch and Furniture beetles burrow as larvae in structural timber, riddling and weakening it, and do an immense amount of damage.

Living plants are the food of thousands of beetle species, and some of them have become very serious pests of agriculture. The notorious Colorado beetle is one of these. When first discovered it was a rare and localized insect feeding on buffalo burr in the Rocky Mountains. Buffalo burr is in the same family of plants as potato and unfortunately the beetle found the potato plant a palatable and wholesome alternative diet. Now it is spread over a large area of North America and Europe and its control is a very costly business. The Cotton Boll weevil is another extremely harmful beetle; as are the various species of cockchafers which feed as larvae on roots underground and as beetles on the foliage of trees and bushes.

All of the so-called fire-flies and glow-worms are really beetles. They are active during the night and their remarkable luminous organs enable the sexes to recognize and find one another. The songs of the crickets and cicadas and the distinctive scents of many moths serve the same purpose.

No beetles, and indeed very few insects have become adapted for life in the sea, but large numbers of them inhabit fresh waters. Some are predatory, feeding both as larvae and adults on other insects and even on tadpoles and small fish. Other water beetles are plant feeders, but all of them have remained air breathers and use various devices for collecting air from the surface and storing it for respiration under the water. The very widespread predatory Diving beetles (*Dytiscidae*) float with the tail at the surface, taking in air which is stored under the wing-cases or elytra. The little Whirligig beetles skate actively on the surface of the water.

Beetles are second only to the butterflies and moths in popularity with insect collectors. They are easy to preserve, and their enormous diversity makes them fascinating to collect, though rather difficult to identify accurately. They are not as uniformly beautiful as butterflies, but many beetles are sufficiently remarkable in appearance to excite admiration. Among these are the horned stag-beetles and the longicorns with their very long antennae. The metallic wood-boring beetles (*Buprestidae*) include many species with iridescent green, bronze and blue colours sufficiently brilliant to give them a place among the most exquisite of all insects. They are not only esteemed by collectors, but also by the native people of many tropical regions, who collect them and use their brilliantly shining elytra to make necklaces and decoration.

Previous page: left:
Jester Bug *(Graphosoma italicum).* The name of this insect is an apt comment on its appearance, but its conspicuous colours and pattern certainly have no purpose of arousing amusement or admiration. Even quite gentle handling causes it to emit a strong and very unpleasant smell, and its striking coloration has without doubt been evolved as a warning to birds and other insectivorous animals that it is inedible and best left alone. It inhabits southern Europe and this one was photographed in Spain.

Previous page: right:
Winged Aphid. Most kinds of aphids or greenfly produce both winged and wingless individuals in the course of their breeding. The ones that can fly are so small and light that they may be carried great distances by wind currents, even over seas and oceans. Most of the breeding of aphids is parthenogenetic – that is, the females produce offspring without mating – but in the autumn males and females mate and the eggs are laid on the bark of trees where they overwinter. The parthenogenetically-produced offspring of aphids do not hatch from eggs, but are born alive. The species shown here is found on nettles.

Above:
Juniper Shield-bug *(Cyphostethus tristriatus).* Shield-bugs are so called from the resemblance of some of them, in outline, to a heraldic shield, and the species shown here is an example. They also look rather like beetles, but the beak-like mouth-parts, designed for piercing and sucking, distinguish them immediately. This species is mainly confined to juniper trees growing in lowland country or on chalk downs, and the berries are its principal food. It is also found occasionally on cypress. It is widespread in Europe and not uncommon in southern England.

Top right:
Planthopper *(Naethus vitripennis).* The bugs of this family, the *Fulgoridae*, are also known by the inappropriate name of 'Lantern flies', apparently because a large tropical American species was mistakenly described as being luminous when first discovered. Fulgorid bugs are very diverse in appearance, and many of them produce fine waxy filaments on various parts of their bodies. This is a young individual or nymph and has a remarkable tuft of these filaments growing from its tail. It inhabits South Africa.

Right:
Periodical Cicada *(Magicicada).* Until recently it has been supposed that only one species of *Magicicada* lives in the United States, but close study has now revealed that there are six, three requiring 13 years to complete their development, the other three living for 17 years. Male cicadas 'sing' by means of a pair of rapidly vibrating membranes inside the body and have by far the loudest voices of any insects. The periodical cicadas of any particular region all hatch at the same time, gathering together in noisy swarms, and then disappear again for 13 or 17 years according to the species.

Left:
Water-cricket *(Velia caprai)*. The English name of this insect is unfortunate as it is not a cricket but a bug of the sub-order *Heteroptera*. It floats and runs on the surface film of water that is shaded and slowly flowing. If you watch a woodland stream with pools you will almost always see water-crickets skimming across the surface. It preys on insects or spiders that fall onto the water, and is guided to them by the ripples resulting from their struggles and, at close range, by its eyesight. It is common all over Britain and Europe.

Below:
Spotted Longhorn Beetle *(Strangalia maculata)*. The longhorn beetles *(Cerambycidae)* are noted for their very long antennae, which are three or four times the length of the body in some species. The Spotted Longhorn is common in England and Europe and often seen on flowers. It varies greatly in the amounts of black and yellow colour. Its larva feeds on dead wood. The specimen photographed is just taking to flight, and the hind-wings are in process of being unfolded, while the wing-cases or elytra are held out on either side.

Right:
A beetle of the family *Buprestidae* from South Africa. The photograph shows a female laying her eggs on the bark of a tree. This group of beetles have two features which make them noticeable; one is that their larvae tunnel in the wood of living trees, sometimes killing the tree and often spoiling the timber, so foresters regard them with hostility. On the other hand some species, especially tropical ones, are extremely beautiful, with brilliant metallic blue, green or gold wing-cases, which are often used as ornaments.

Following page: top left:
Lunate Ladybird *(Chilomenes lunata)*. This very beautiful ladybird lives in the grassland or highveld of South Africa, and this individual was photographed in the act of devouring aphids. All over the world these little beetles do good service by destroying aphids, scale insects and other types of plant lice which, if unchecked, would severely restrict the growth of almost all vegetation, including, of course, the crops we grow for food. The larvae of ladybirds feed in the same way as the beetles, but are even more voracious.

Below:
Acorn Weevil *(Balaninus venosus).* The weevils (Curculionidae) are the most numerous of all the beetles, about 40,000 species being known. Many of them are serious pests of agriculture and of stored products. Most weevils have the fore-part of the head elongated to form a snout, and in some, as in the Acorn Weevil, it is remarkably long and slender. The antennae are half-way along the snout and the jaws are at its tip. The female uses her jaws to drill holes in acorns and then turns round and inserts her eggs, one to each acorn, and the larva feeds inside it.

Right:
Cockchafer or **Maybug** *(Melolontha melolontha).* This large and very harmful beetle is common in Britain and extends eastward to the area north of the Black Sea. The larvae are large white grubs

27

which feed on the roots of grass and other plants, including seedling trees. The beetles fly at night and rest by day on the branches of trees and bushes, feeding on the leaves. It is recorded that 80 bushels of beetles were once gathered on a single farm. The curious fan-like antennae of the male are well shown in the photograph.

Below:
Thick-legged Flower Beetle *(Oedemera nobilis)*. This handsome beetle is often seen in southern England on sunny days feeding on the nectar of wild flowers. The greatly thickened femora or thighs of the hind-legs are a feature of the male and presumably have some sexual significance, but their actual function is not known; all the legs are normal and slender in the female. The larva feeds inside the stems of plants.

Left:
Carrion Beetle *(Necrodes littoralis).* Several kinds of beetles feed, both as larvae and adults, on carcasses of animals. The well-known Burying Beetles or Sexton Beetles actually enter small animals and birds, but the species shown here merely feeds on any dead animal it can find, and also on the maggots of flies that infest carcasses. Beetles that pursue this way of life often become infested with parasitic mites, and this specimen has numbers of them clinging to its legs and body.

Centre:
Oil Beetle *(Meloe majalis).* The strange appearance of the oil beetles is more than matched by their breeding habits. The female becomes greatly swollen and lays thousands of tiny eggs in crevices in the ground. These hatch into active larvae which climb onto plants and seize any hairy insect that approaches. Only those few which happen to attach themselves to a certain kind of wild bee can survive; the rest, and the vast majority, perish. The lucky ones devour the larva of the bee and then subsist on its store of honey and pollen. This is a large southern European species and was photographed in Spain.

Bottom left:
Dung Beetles or **Scarabs** *(Gymnopleurus virens).* This South African beetle is allied to the Sacred Scarab of Egypt and the Mediterranean countries, and has similar

habits. These insects collect the dung of animals, shape it into a ball and roll it away to a place where the soil is suitable for burying it. The beetles often work in pairs, and they both feed on the dung themselves and lay eggs on it, providing their larvae with a secure underground store of food. Their habits are useful both for hygiene and in fertilizing the soil.

Right:
Stag Beetles *(Lucanus cervus).* This is the largest British beetle and very well known although it is not really very common. Only the males have the great antler-like mandibles. Those of the smaller female are short and much more effective for biting. The males use their jaws as a threat, opening them wide when molested, and also employ them in rather ineffective combats between each other, as these two are doing. The larvae live for several years in dead tree stumps.

Below:
Whirligig Beetles *(Gyrinus).* There are several species of whirligigs, very similar to each other in appearance. They spend their lives weaving mazily about on the surface film of the water in ponds and canals; often large groups of them gather together. If frightened they dive under the surface, but soon come up again. Their eyes are divided into two parts, an upper and a lower; the lower part is submerged, and it seems likely that it is adapted for seeing under water while the upper part functions in the air.

Butterflies and Moths

It is rather unfortunate that we must always say 'butterflies and moths' in English to denote the Lepidoptera; most other languages have a word for the order as a whole. Although the division is unnatural from the point of view of entomology, it is understandable when one considers that the bright day-flying butterflies were probably the first insects to be regarded by man with feelings other than disgust and hostility. The bright yellow Brimstone butterfly (*Gonepteryx rhamni*) is one of the first to appear in spring in northern Europe and to proclaim that the hardships of winter are nearly over. These were very real only two or three hundred years ago, and people welcomed the gaily coloured harbinger of warmth and sunshine and called it the butter-coloured fly; and that is how we came to speak of butterflies.

They form one group of the Lepidoptera or scale-winged insects; the other group, consisting of moths, is much more diverse and numerous. The more obvious differences between them are not really clear cut. Butterflies fly by day, but so do many moths. Most butterflies, but not all, rest with the wings laid together upright over the back and very few moths adopt this posture. All butterflies have the ends of the antennae thickened and club-shaped, in moths the antennae vary in form but are only rarely thickened at the ends. The matter is complicated further by the fact that the Skippers (*Hesperiodae*), traditionally regarded as butterflies, are not at all closely related to any of the rest of the butterflies and are now often excluded from butterfly books.

Two obvious characteristics distinguish the Lepidoptera from the rest of the insects. Firstly, as the name implies, the wings are covered with scales. These appear like powder when the insect is handled, but when in place can be seen, with magnification, to be arranged in rows, overlapping one another like tiles on a roof. Each scale is of some particular colour and together they make up the intricate and beautiful patterns that adorn the wings, just as small self-coloured pieces make up a mosaic. No other insects have such an effective mode of wing coloration and it is undoubtedly used as a means of visual recognition between the sexes, as camouflage and as warnings that the insect is dangerous or unpleasant to eat. Examples are shown in the last chapter.

Their other distinguishing character is the remarkable tongue or proboscis, which may be twice or more the length of the head and body. The maxillae, one of the paired elements of the mouth-parts in primitive insects, have evolved to form greatly elongated tubes which lie side by side like the two barrels of a shot gun. When not in use the organ is coiled up under the head and looks rather like the hairspring of a watch. It is used for sucking up liquid food, most usually the nectar of flowers, but some tropical moths have the proboscis stiff and sharp and use it to pierce the rind of fruits. A Malayan moth (*Calyptra eustrigata*) has recently been shown to be a blood-sucker, stabbing its proboscis through the skin of large animals, including buffaloes, and men if given the opportunity.

Most of the larvae of Lepidoptera feed on the leaves of plants and are easy and pleasant to keep in captivity. This is rewarding both to observe the transformations from larva to pupa and pupa to perfect insect and as a means of obtaining perfect specimens for a collection. With the first object in view butterflies are better than moths because they generally turn into pupae in the open and not enclosed in a cocoon. The caterpillar suspends itself by means of silk, which is spun by all lepidopterous larvae, and then its skin splits behind the head and slides back to reveal the pupa or chrysalis underneath. Shrugging and wriggling movements cause the skin to slide back to the tail and its dried and crumpled remains eventually drop off.

The hatching or eclosion of a butterfly from its pupa is a far more spectacular performance. Photography has made it familiar and has perhaps blunted our sense of wonder at one of the lovelier miracles of natural history. Even so, when you have just watched a butterfly emerge it is hard to believe that the broad, patterned wings were packed into so small a space a few minutes before. Breeding butterflies is indeed well worth the small amount of trouble it entails.

As we have said, most of the larvae feed on the leaves of plants. The majority eat away the leaf from the edge, only rasping away the surface of the leaf when newly hatched and very small. Some of the very minute moths spend their period of feeding and growing inside the leaf, eating out the tissue between its upper and lower layers. Light coloured markings looking like rivers on a map can often be seen on leaves, and these are the mines made by these minute caterpillars. As the larva eats its way along the course of its mine it grows, causing the mine to widen gradually up to its point of exit and enhancing the resemblance to a river. Some other small larvae, especially of flies, feed in the same way.

There are also larvae of moths which tunnel in the stems and roots of plants, and even in solid wood, the Goat moth (*Cossus cossus*) being a well-known example. Others are scavengers in bees' and wasps' nests and some are predators. The most remarkable of these are the larvae of certain Blue butterflies (*Lycaenidae*) which are carried into their nests by ants. The caterpillars secrete a sweet liquid which the ants greatly relish. They pay for it by sacrifice of their own children,

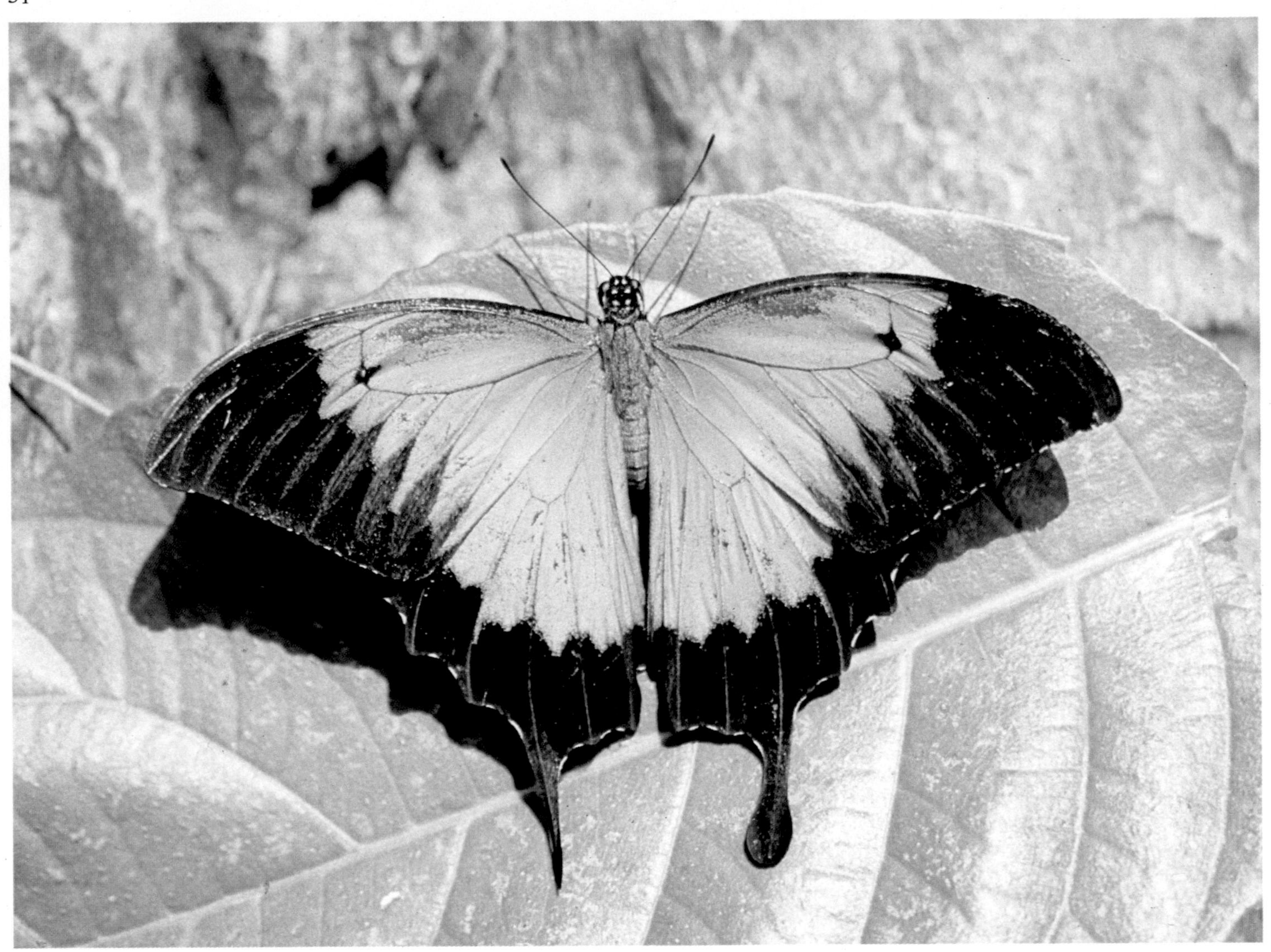

for the larvae and pupae of the ants are the caterpillars' food. One small group of Blues, represented in North America by the Harvester (*Feniseca tarquinius*), has joined the honourable company of aphis eaters.

We have mentioned that butterfly pupae are almost always exposed while those of moths are hidden away in cocoons, often underground. Although moths are so much more diverse than butterflies, their pupae, in outward appearance, are far more uniform. Almost all of them look like brown or black bullets, very hard to identify until the moth emerges. Butterfly pupae are extremely diverse in appearance, often adapted to look like twigs, hanging dead leaves or parts of live green leaves. In some tropical butterflies these resemblances are fantastically precise. Their exposed situation makes it necessary for butterfly pupae to be adapted for concealment; those of moths have no need for it.

The aristocrats of the butterfly world are surely the Swallowtails. To see them in their glory one must go to the tropics, to the perennially green, towering rain forest, which is so rapidly and tragically being destroyed. There they are the largest, brightest butterflies, and the great Birdwing Swallowtails of New Guinea and the surrounding islands are the biggest and most splendid of all. Only the males are vividly coloured, metallic green, blue or orange, and only the females are really large. The sombre brown and white female of Queen Alexandra's Birdwing is the world's largest butterfly with a wing span that may reach eleven inches.

Among moths the *Saturniidae*, the emperors and atlas moths, rank as the swallowtails do among the butterflies. They also are mainly tropical. Only one occurs in Britain and half-a-dozen throughout Europe, but in North America, north of Mexico, between 50 and 60 are found. In the tropical forests they abound and include some of the largest of all Lepidoptera, the Giant Atlas of tropical Asia and the huge Hercules moth of New Guinea and northern Australia, whose wings have a surface area of about 40 square inches. The hawk-moths too are aristocrats. Many are very large and they share with the big dragonflies the distinction of having the fastest and most powerful flight of all insects.

At the other end of the scale the so-called Microlepidoptera are worthy of more notice than they generally receive. These are the small and minute moths that most collectors find too troublesome to pin and mount and to identify. They are accordingly designated 'micros' and neglected. They are indeed very hard to prepare for a collection, and so small that a lens is required to appreciate their often fantastic beauty. They are ideal subjects for close-up photography, which modern apparatus renders less and less difficult to do. Such photographs can be enlarged for easy viewing and depict the tiny insects in perfect conditions, especially if they are bred. Few of them have ever been photographed alive and the field is wide open for any ambitious nature photographer.

Previous page: left:
Achemon Sphinx *(Eumorpha achemon).* Over forty species of hawkmoths or sphinx moths are found in America north of Mexico, many of them being tropical or subtropical species at the northern limit of their range. The Achemon Sphinx is one of these, an inhabitant of South America and the West Indies and extending northward into the southern USA. It is a beautiful insect with delicate pink hind-wings, which are concealed when it is at rest. The caterpillar feeds on grape-vines and Amelopsis.

Previous page: right:
Blue Mountain Swallowtail *(Papilio ulysses).* Many large and splendid butterflies are found in the rain forest of tropical Australia and the great island of New Guinea, whose animal life is similar to that of Australia, and this beautiful swallowtail is one of them. On the mainland it extends south to Sarina in Queensland. It flies fast and high, but males can be lured to ground level by exposing a bright blue object, best of all a mounted specimen of the butterfly itself. Females are not attracted and can only occasionally be seen in close view when they visit low-growing flowers.

Below and right:
Privet Hawkmoth *(Sphinx ligustri).* This is the largest native British moth; the Convolvulus and Deaths-head Hawkmoths are larger still but are migratory visitors from the south and cannot complete their life cycle in Britain in the open. The hind-wings of the Privet Hawkmoth, concealed when the moth is at rest, are pink banded with black. The curious resting attitude of the caterpillar has been likened to that of the Egyptian Sphinx and is the origin of the generic name of this species. The name Sphinx Moth is used in America as a general term for the Hawkmoths.

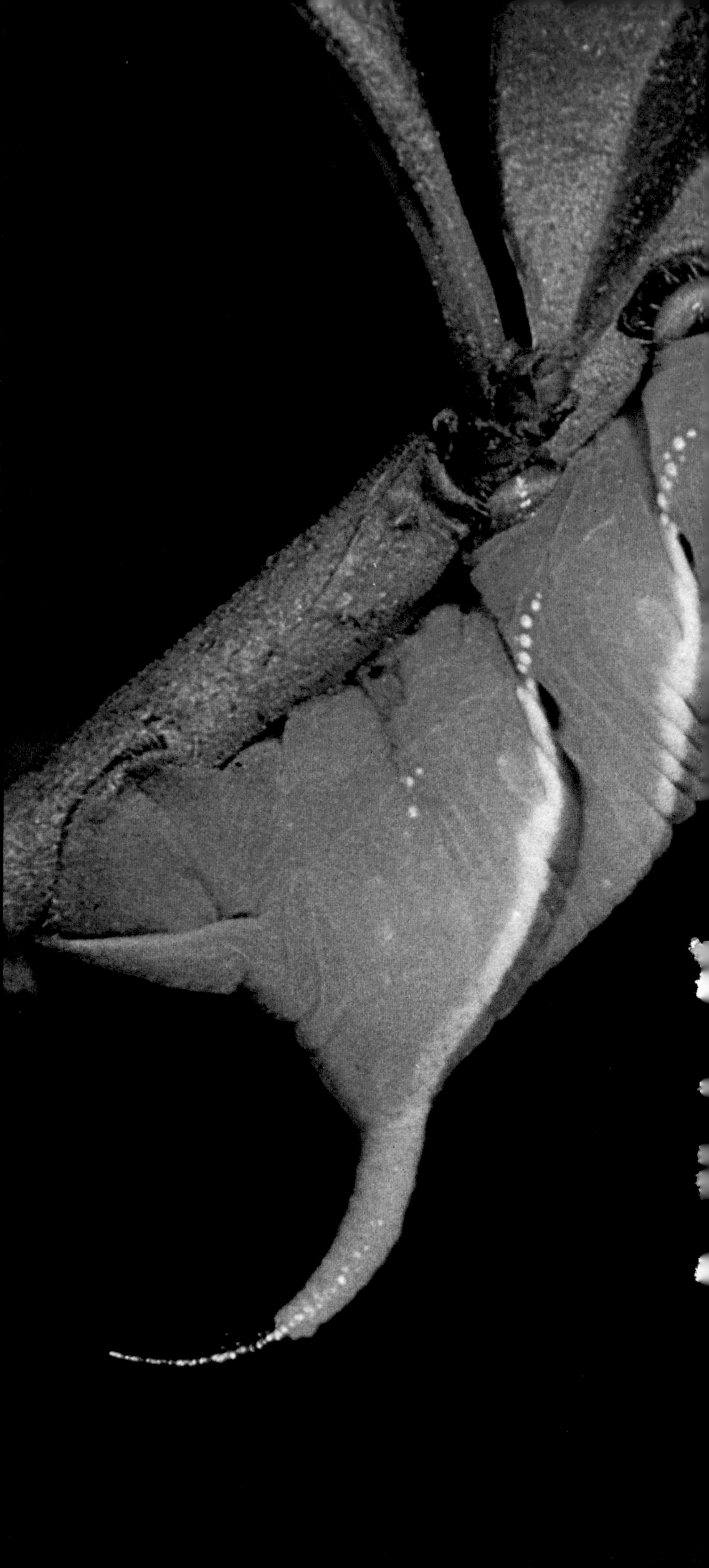

Above:
Red Lacewing Butterfly *(Cethosia chrysippe).* It is the pattern on the underside of the wings, combined with the scalloped edges which gives this name to the beautiful Lacewing butterflies. They occur from India through Malaysia and Indonesia to northern Australia. The caterpillars feed on Adenia, a creeper of the passion-flower family and they are conspicuously coloured and gregarious when at rest. The species shown here is Australian and the photograph was taken in Queensland.

Left:
Marbled White Butterfly *(Melanargia galathea).* The family to which this butterfly belongs, the Satyridae, consists mostly of light or dark brown insects with small eye-like spots on the wings, but otherwise not conspicuously ornamented. The prettily chequered Marbled Whites form an exception to this general rule. There are several species found in Europe, western Asia and North Africa of which this is the most common, and the only species found in Britain. The larva lives on grasses.

Right:
Peacock Butterfly *(Inachis io).* This very distinctive butterfly is common from Britain all through temperate Europe and Asia to Japan, but does not extend into America. The larva feeds on nettle and the butterfly hibernates through the winter, sheltering in a cave or hollow tree or, in these days, more usually in an attic or out-house. In the warm days of spring it emerges and lays its eggs. A peacock, tamed and artificially fed, has been known to live, as a butterfly, for eleven months.

Left:
Skipper Butterfly *(Metisella orientalis).* The Skippers differ so much from all other butterflies that they are now given the status of a super-family on their own, and some of the recent books on butterflies exclude them altogether. They resemble moths in having thick muscular bodies and rapid buzzing flight, but are almost without exception day-fliers and lovers of bright sunshine. The Skippers or Hesperidae are distributed all over the world and most abundant in tropical America. This is a tropical African species and was photographed in Uganda.

Below left:
Golden Emperor Moth *(Loepa katinka).* Perhaps the most beautiful of all the Saturniids, this species is found in India and the far-eastern tropics. Its wings display the eye-like markings characteristic of the family. The moths sit at rest with their wings outspread, and it is possible that the effect of a mask or face which is produced may alarm birds, which have good reason to fear such predators as cats and owls. The Golden Emperor can be bred in captivity if the larva is given the leaves of grape vine or virginia creeper.

Right:
Thicket Hairstreak *(Mitoura spinetorum).* The Hairstreaks are allied to the Blues but are generally less brightly coloured. Their name refers to the fine pale line that runs across the underside of both wings, and is particularly well seen in this species. Another characteristic feature of the Hairstreaks is the presence of appendages or 'tails' on the hind-wing. In some tropical species these reach fantastic lengths. The Thicket Hairstreak is a North American butterfly found in the western States.

Below right:
Purple-edged Copper *(Palaeochrysophanus hippothoe).* The Coppers form a third group of the Lycaenid butterflies, in addition to the Blues and Hairstreaks. They are characteristic of the temperate regions of the Northern Hemisphere, and the Purple-edged Copper is one of the most beautiful of all of them. It is widespread in Europe and frequents boggy places in the lowlands and up to 5,000 feet in the mountains. This one was photographed at about this altitude in the French Pyrenees.

Left:
Indian Moon Moth *(Actias selene).* The beautiful Moon Moths form a very distinct group within the family Saturniidae. The long tails on their hind-wings recall those of some of the Swallowtail butterflies. This is an Indian moth, one of a number of species of Moon Moths that inhabit the Oriental region. A similar species, *Actias luna*, is found in North America. Natural history dealers can usually supply living material of these moths in their early stages. The Indian species will eat leaves of rhododendron, hawthorn and plum, while walnut or birch is recommended for *Actias luna.*

Below:
Edwards's Atlas Moth *(Attacus edwardsi).* The family Saturniidae forms a distinctive group of moths, mostly of large size, the biggest of them being the largest moths known. They are often referred to as 'giant silkmoths', but it must be remembered that the silkmoth of commerce, *Bombyx mori*, is not a Saturniid. The few Saturniids that produce usable silk are of minor importance. The Atlas Moths include some of the largest members of the family. The species shown here is a native of India.

Right:
Raja Brooke's Birdwing *(Trogonoptera brookiana).* One of the most beautiful of the tropical Oriental butterflies, this species was discovered in Borneo in 1855 by the English explorer and naturalist A R Wallace, and he named it in honour of Sir James Brooke, the first of the White rulers of Sarawak. The female is seldom seen but the males often gather in numbers on moist ground by rivers or at springs of mineralized water, presenting a magnificent spectacle, as shown in this photograph. The butterfly is confined to the Malay Peninsula and the islands of Borneo and Sumatra.

Left:
Plain Tiger Butterfly *(Danaus chrysippus).* This tropical relative of the Monarch Butterfly has a very wide range, from Africa through Asia to Australia. Plain Tiger is the name by which it goes in Asia; in Africa it is called the African Monarch, and in Australia the Lesser Wanderer. The one shown here was photographed in Queensland. Like that of the Monarch its caterpillar feeds on poisonous milkweeds and birds avoid attacking the butterflies. The larvae of the *Danaus* species also escape accidental destruction because grazing animals are reluctant to eat the plants.

Below left:
Monarch Butterfly *(Danaus plexippus).* The North American Monarch is a famous butterfly both as a migrant and as an example of a butterfly protected from predation by poisonous qualities derived from its food plant. Butterflies have been caught, marked and then released and finally picked up again over 2,000 miles away. Since man has established the milkweeds *(Asclepias)* in Africa, Australia and elsewhere the Monarch has invaded these territories, sometimes flying enormous distances over the oceans in order to do so. There seems to be no doubt that they can cross the Atlantic from America to Europe.

Bottom left:
Mazarine Blue *(Cyaniris semiargus).* The Blues, Coppers and Hairstreaks of the family Lycaenidae occur in great diversity all over the world, extending from the tropics to the Arctic regions and far above the timber line on the mountains. This is a common species in Europe and once occurred in Britain, but is now extinct. It is found from sea level to 7,000-8,000 feet in the mountains and can often be seen congregating at muddy places on paths in order to suck up moisture. This one was photographed in the Pyrenees mountains in Spain.

Right:
Tiger Swallowtail *(Papilio glaucus).* The big yellow and black Tiger Swallowtail is one of the most familiar North American butterflies, and ranges from the latitude of Hudson Bay in Canada to that of Florida and Texas. In the south a dark brown form of the female occurs, forming as much as 50 per cent of the population in some areas. The dark-coloured female is believed to be a mimic of the Pipe-vine Swallowtail *(Papilio philenor)* as it resembles this species and has a closely similar geographical range. The larva of the Pipe-vine Swallowtail feeds on Aristolochia, a poisonous creeper, and the poison of the plant is retained by the insect and makes it distasteful to birds even when it becomes a butterfly. The Tiger Swallowtail feeds as a caterpillar on birch, poplar, ash and other trees.

Below:
Elephant Hawkmoth *(Deilephila elpenor).* The enormous compound eye typical of this species is well shown in this photograph. Another interesting feature appears, which is the apparatus that links the fore- and hind-wings together in flight. The element that can be seen is the pale coloured strap (retinaculum) near the base of the fore-wing, which wraps round a slender bristle (frenulum) on the hind-wing. The name 'Elephant' does not, of course, refer to any feature of the delicately beautiful moth, but to the caterpillar, the foremost part of whose body can be extended so that it looks like a trunk. It feeds on various species of willow herb.

Below right:
Royal Walnut Moth *(Citheronia regalis).* Although included in the family Saturniidae this American moth differs greatly in appearance from the majority of them, and its attitude at rest is also not that of a normal Saturniid. It is found in the eastern States of the USA. Its remarkable larva is five inches long when fully grown and has several pairs of long spines on the back, just behind the head. It is coloured green, marked with white or yellow rectangles and bright blue or scarlet patches and has come to be known as the 'Hickory Horned Devil'. Walnut and butternut are the most usual food plants.

Bottom right:
White-lined Sphinx *(Hyles lineata).* The most widely distributed of the New World Hawkmoths, this species occurs over most of both North and South America. A curious dwarf race of it is found in the Galapagos Islands. It has a very close relative in Africa, the Striped Hawkmoth *(Hyles livornica)*, which differs in the pattern of white lines on the thorax. In some summers this species migrates northward into Europe in large numbers. Unlike most Hawkmoths, both these moths feed as larvae on a wide variety of plants.

Right:
Promethea Moth *(Callosamia promethea).* This handsome Saturniid moth inhabits the eastern region of the United States and ranges north to Ontario and Quebec. The male and female are very different in appearance, and the male flies by day, the female by night. The coloration of the male is consistent with the view that it is a mimic of the Pipe-vine Swallowtail Butterfly *(Papilio philenor)*, which is distasteful to predators and, of course, also a day flier. The caterpillar of the Promethea Moth feeds on a wide variety of trees, including apple, plum, cherry and willow.

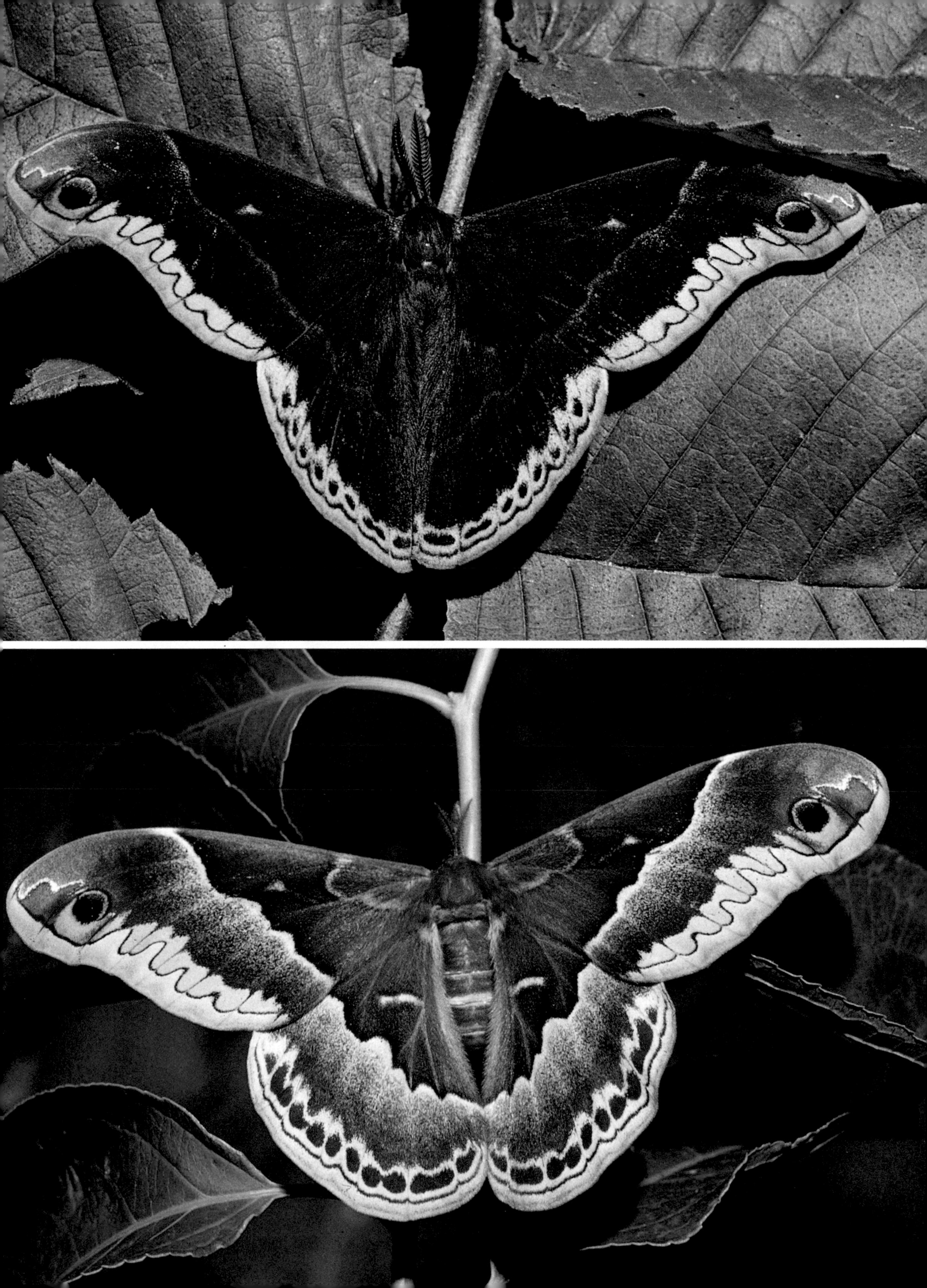

Left:
Bordered Beauty Moth *(Epione repandaria).* The large family of moths known as Geometridae consists mainly of fairly small, delicate insects which sit at rest with the wings extended and flattened on each side of the body. Their larvae are peculiar in having legs only at the front and hind ends so that they walk with a looping action, alternately arching and straightening the body. The name 'Geometridae' meaning 'earth measurers' refers to this. The caterpillar of this species feeds on poplar and willow and is shown on page 68.

Below left:
Beautiful Chinamark Moth *(Nymphula stagnata).* This prettily patterned small moth is common in Britain among vegetation growing beside ponds and stagnant or slowly flowing ditches and canals. Its larva is wholly aquatic, feeding under the water on pondweed and other plants and breathing by means of gills. About three days after hatching it makes a flat oval case out of pieces of the leaf of the food plant and inhabits this until it is

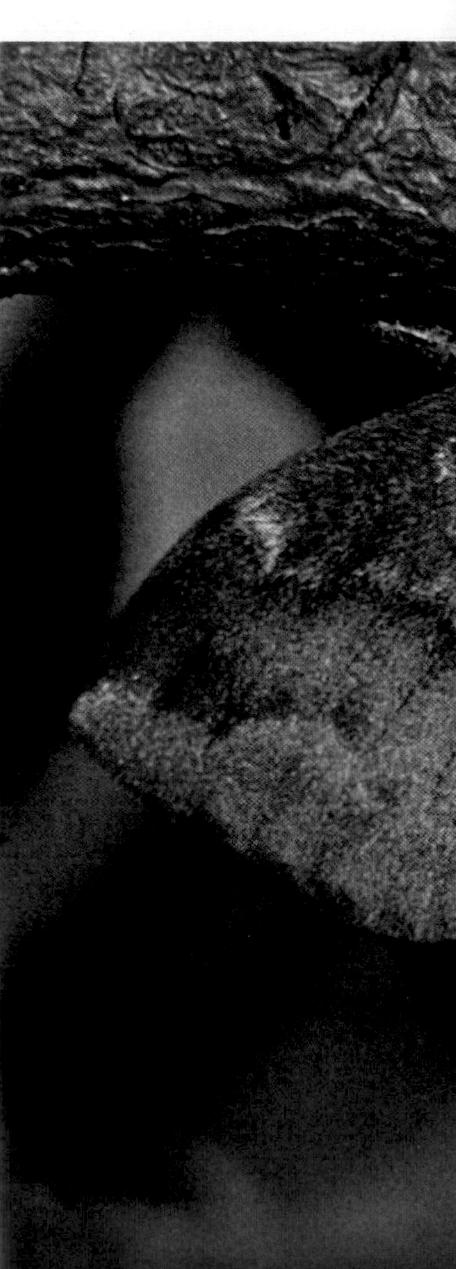

ready to pupate. The pupa is enclosed in a greyish-white silken cocoon attached to the stem of a plant an inch or so above water level.

Bottom left:
White Plume Moth *(Pterophorus pentadactylus).* The Plume Moths form a very distinct group in which the body and legs are slender and the wings nearly always divided into fingers or lobes, each of which is bordered with delicate hairs, so that it looks rather like the feather of a bird. The fore-wings are split into two lobes, the hind-wings into three. When at rest the White Plume and its relatives always stand on the two front pairs of legs and lay the hindmost pair back against the abdomen, apparently making no use of them as legs at all. The larva feeds on the common small convolvulus called bindweed.

Right:
Geoffroy's Tubic *(Oecophora geofrella).* This tiny moth, barely a centimetre long, has been chosen to illustrate the fantastic beauty of some of the so-called Microlepidoptera. It flies in May and June along hedgerows and in open woods, settling in the sunshine on leaves. The larva feeds in the early months of the year on decayed wood. The British must be the only nation for which names have been devised in the language of the country for all the Lepidoptera occurring there. Over 2,400 names go to make up this unique vocabulary.

Below:
Io or **Bullseye Moth** *(Automeris io).* The moths of the genus *Automeris* have leaf-like fore-wings and very conspicuous eye-spots on the hind-wings. A large number of species live in the South and Central American tropics, and this one has evidently spread northward, in the course of its evolution, extending through the United States to southern Canada. Another species, *Automeris iris*, is found in the southern USA. The caterpillars of these moths are covered with fine spines which are poisonous and can sting severely. That of *Automeris io* can be bred on leaves of poplar, willow, birch and other trees.

Flies

Just as bugs are to the entomologist a particular order of insects, so are flies not just any insect with wings, but an order, the *Diptera*, with very well defined characteristics. The chief of these, the one that their name signifies, is the possession of a single pair of wings, and for greater precision they are often called in English the 'two-winged' or 'true' flies.

In place of hind-wings, and modified from them in the course of evolution, flies have a pair of small knobbed stalks called halteres. They are joined to the thorax in the same way as the wings and vibrate up and down at the same speed as the wings do. Acting on rather the same principle as a gyroscope they serve as balancers, keeping the insect on a level course of flight. If the halteres are removed from a fly, it flies in an uncoordinated way and crashes to the ground like an uncontrolled aeroplane.

Some of the smaller flies vibrate their wings at almost unbelievable speeds. Mosquitoes perform about 600 up-and-down beats per second, and a minute midge called *Forcipomyia* achieves a frequency of 1,000 beats a second. In mosquitoes the pitch of the sound produced when the insect flies provides a means of recognition between the sexes of particular species.

Some of the more advanced flies have the most perfectly controlled flight achieved by any insect. Hover-flies are able to stand motionless in the air like tiny helicopters. In still air this would be remarkable, but the air out of doors is never still, there is always some lateral drift and irregular eddies, and yet the fly manages to maintain its position. It probably does this by using its large and efficient eyes to register changes in its position relative to objects in its vicinity, automatically using minute adjustments in the action of its wings to correct shifts due to air movements. Hover-flies are one of the few groups within the *Diptera* that can be regarded as attractive insects, and at the same time many of them are useful and very few do any harm. The useful species are those which join forces with the Ladybird beetles and Lacewings in keeping down the numbers of aphids. Their larvae are small and slug-like, usually tapering towards one end, and they can often be found on plants where aphids are present. Remember that not every caterpillar-like creature on your rose bushes is devouring the leaves. The flies themselves almost all feed on the nectar of flowers and assist in the pollination of many cultivated plants.

Unfortunately the Hover-flies are the only conspicuous group of flies which we can regard with approval and pleasure. Vast numbers among the other groups are entirely neutral so far as man is concerned and pass unnoticed, but a small proportion are among the most dangerous of our insect enemies.

Not many are serious agricultural pests, though the names of the Cabbage Root fly, Onion fly and Wheat Bulb fly speak for their activities, and the 'leather-jackets', the larvae of the Crane-flies or Daddy-long-legs may seriously damage lawns and pasture. It is as carriers of disease that flies exact an immense toll of human misery and death. One of the worst is the common House-fly, whose diversified appetite leads it to fly from a meal of crude sewage to alight on a plate of sweet cakes exposed for sale. It has the unpleasing habit of regurgitating liquid from its last meal in order to dissolve the substance of the next one, and not much imagination is required to see what will happen in places where food is left exposed and hygiene is rudimentary. Gastro-intestinal diseases of all kinds flourish in these conditions, especially dysentery, and infant and child mortality will be distressingly high.

The part played by mosquitoes in transmitting malaria is of quite a different nature. Here the insect, and only the female, feeds on animal and human blood, piercing the skin with mouth-parts adapted for the purpose. If the victim of the bite is infected with malaria, some of the organisms causing the disease will be sucked up by the mosquito. In its body they will undergo certain transformations which end in their crowding into the insect's salivary glands. When a mosquito bites it always injects some saliva as an anti-coagulant, before sucking the blood. A mosquito that has bitten an infected person is therefore almost bound to transfer the infection to others when it again seeks a blood meal. Malaria is not carried by just any mosquito; only certain species of the genus *Anopheles* can provide conditions for the malarial parasite to develop in their bodies. Anti-malarial measures therefore largely depend on careful study of the biology of the carrier species followed by action taken against them. The most effective is the destruction of their breeding grounds. All mosquito larvae breed in water and the draining of lakes and swamps has played a large part in eradicating malaria from populated areas.

In tropical jungles spraying of inside house walls with DDT has proved effective, as the mosquitoes settle on the walls after feeding. This method is complicated by the fact that mutations of mosquitoes occur which are resistant to DDT and natural selection soon establishes them as the dominant *Anopheles* population. Increase of strength of the insecticide may have a temporary effect, but further mutation will restore the balance, and too much DDT is environmentally very dangerous.

Other diseases are carried by mosquitoes of different kinds. Yellow fever is caused by a virus which is conveyed by mosquitoes of the genus *Aedes*. Other biting flies, such as Sand-flies, Black-flies

and the notorious Tsetse fly convey a variety of diseases. The Tsetse fly, which is confined to Africa, south of the Sahara, carries the organism responsible for the terrible human disease sleeping sickness and also the disease of cattle and horses called Nagana. During the long period when land transport virtually depended on horses, great areas of Africa could only be traversed on foot, with human carriers for baggage, and the limit of agriculture was laborious toil with a hoe.

There are other flies which are pests of domestic animals rather than of man himself. The larvae of Bot flies live in the nasal cavities of various animals and the Warble flies lay eggs on the beasts' legs, their larvae thereafter penetrating the skin and travelling, as they feed, inside the body. When ready to form pupae they make their way through the skin and drop to the ground. Besides damaging the animal's health they leave its hide pitted with holes, which much reduces its value as a source of leather. Horse-flies torment grazing beasts with their biting and can be a serious nuisance to people walking in woods or on moors, but they are not known to transmit disease.

A number of flies attack other insects and so, to some extent, benefit man. The fierce Robber flies hunt their prey rather as dragonflies do, but impale the victim on a sharp proboscis as they have no jaws with which to chew it up. Far more deadly are the *Tachinidae*, flies which lay their eggs on caterpillars, or on the leaves on which they feed, and whose larvae live as internal parasites. They slowly devour the living tissue until the host is full-sized, or even has pupated, and then put an end to its life by eating the vital organs. This way of life is paralleled by the Ichneumon wasps which we shall meet in the next chapter.

One tiny fly has benefited mankind in a curious way. The Fruit-flies of the genus *Drosophila* have been found so suitable for research on heredity that the modern science of genetics is largely based on the study of them. They are very easy to breed, complete their life cycle rapidly and mutations frequently occur among them. Also they have only four chromosomes in the cell nucleus, an abnormally low number which simplifies work on them, and the chromosomes of the salivary glands are relatively gigantic, making ideal material for microscopic study. The pioneer in this work, and one of the greatest of all geneticists, was the American biologist T H Morgan.

Previous page: left:
Hover-fly *(Syrphus ribesii).* No insects have more perfect control over their flight than hover-flies. Their ability to remain poised in the air in one place must involve constant adjustment of their rapidly vibrating wings to eddies and air currents. The most sophisticated of helicopters works no better than a hover-fly. Many of them are attractively coloured, but the reason for this is almost certainly that they are mimics of wasps and bees, which advertise their ability to sting by warning coloration. This hover-fly is coloured and marked very like a wasp.

Previous page: right:
Fruit-flies *(Drosophila).* If a bowl of fruit or an unwashed wine glass is left standing in a room tiny flies often appear, seeming to come from nowhere, and settle on it. Close examination usually reveals them as members of the genus *Drosophila*, of which there are many similar species. Those shown here have been attracted by a piece of banana that has begun to decay. *Drosophila* is a famous insect for the curious reason that its breeding habits and genetic constitution make it outstandingly suitable for the experimental study of heredity.

Right:
Robber-fly *(Promachus vagator).* This family of flies, the Asilidae, all live as predators on other insects. The South African example shown here has caught a moth and is sucking its body juices by means of its piercing proboscis. The mode of hunting practised by robber-flies is to sit on a projecting leaf or twig and dash out in pursuit of any insect that flies close by. The victim is killed by the injection of poisonous saliva from the proboscis. The red object on the fly's abdomen is a parasitic mite.

Above:
Stalk-eyed Fly *(Diopsis).* The Diopsid flies are among the real curiosities of the insect world. The compound eyes are borne on long stalks, which are prolongations of the head and have the antennae situated half-way along them, as can be seen in this remarkable photograph of an African species. As the field of view of the eyes hardly overlaps, the stalks do not achieve a stereoscopic or 'range-finder' effect, and the purpose of the stalks is still a mystery. Most of these flies live in the tropics.

Left:
Crane-fly *(Tipula maxima).* The most familiar of the Crane-flies is the common Daddy-long-legs *(Tipula paludosa)*, whose larva is the 'leather-jacket', so destructive of lawns and pastures. The species shown here is also found in Britain and Europe but is relatively uncommon and is much larger, having a wing-span of two-and-a-half inches. Its great size and patterned wings give it a striking appearance. The larva is semi-aquatic and lives in the margins of ponds and streams, sometimes actually under the water. It pupates in drier soil above the water level.

Right:
Hover-fly *(Catabomba pyrastri).* Hover-flies are not only pretty and attractive, many of them are useful as well. The larvae of both this species and *Syrphus ribesii* prey on aphids or greenfly. They are slug-like creatures, tapering towards the head, and may often be found on rose bushes or other garden plants. When attacking an aphid a hover-fly larva seizes it and holds it up, clear of the leaf surface, so that its struggles are unavailing, and it is then sucked dry and its empty skin is discarded. Hover-flies are also important as pollinators of flowers, including those of cultivated fruit trees.

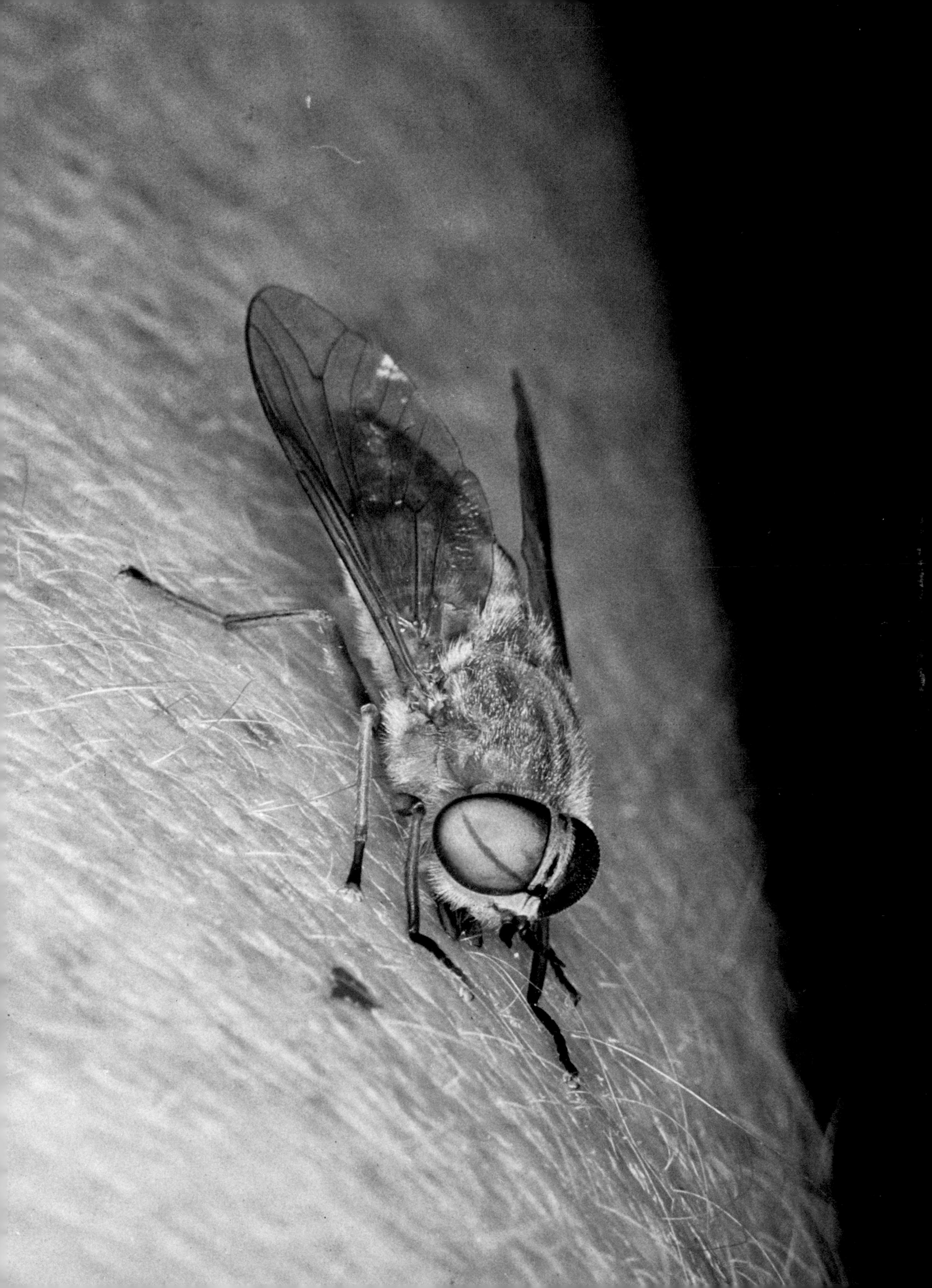

Ants, Bees and Wasps

The insects of the order *Hymenoptera* typically have two pairs of transparent wings, of which the smaller hind pair are connected to the fore-wings by a row of minute hooks, so that the two wings function as one and achieve greater efficiency in flying. Another very general feature among them is the presence of a more or less elongate ovipositor or egg-laying organ at the tip of the abdomen. This has the form of a slender tube down which the egg passes, but in many of the *Hymenoptera* it has lost its primary function and is modified to form a sting. The name *Hymenoptera* means 'membrane-winged' and is not descriptive of the wasps, bees and ants and their relatives in any particular way.

The social wasps, bees and ants are the most highly developed of all insects from the point of view of their behaviour. All ants are social insects, but a far greater number of kinds of bees and wasps lead normal solitary lives than live in organized communities.

Since they are the most primitive members of the group we will consider the sawflies and wood-wasps first. These differ from the rest in having no obvious 'waist' where the thorax joins the abdomen. They all feed on plants, and the female sawflies have the ovipositor toothed like a tiny saw and use it for cutting slits in stems and leaves into which to insert their eggs. Their larvae resemble the caterpillars of butterflies and moths and have a similar way of life, feeding on leaves. They can be distinguished by the greater number, usually eight, of fleshy false legs or prolegs along the body behind the three pairs of jointed true legs. Larvae of *Lepidoptera* never have more than five pairs. The wood-wasps are often large and use their spike-like ovipositors to bore into living wood, in which their larvae tunnel and feed.

A great many *Hymenoptera* have breeding habits similar to those of the Tachinid flies mentioned in the last chapter. The larger ones are known collectively as ichneumon wasps and they insert their eggs into the bodies of various other insects. Their larvae develop as internal parasites, but unlike normal parasites they always kill and completely devour their host when they reach full growth. Some large ichneumons lay only one egg in each victim, others lay a number of them. Some of the minute wasps of the family *Chalcidae* are so small that they can lay a dozen or more eggs in a single EGG of a butterfly or moth and from it a corresponding number of microscopic wasps will in due course appear.

These parasites are by far the most serious enemies that most insects have to contend with, and they are often used in biological control of pests, especially when these have become established in territories far outside their normal range.

The great majority of wasps and bees are of the type known as solitary, that is to say they are not social insects living in communities as the Honey-bee, the more obtrusive wasps and all ants do. The breeding habits of the solitary forms are nevertheless of great interest. After mating the female makes a nest, often in a burrow or hollow plant stem, but sometimes a structure of clay, to accommodate her offspring. In most species the nest is divided into compartments in each of which a store of food is placed and a single egg laid. The quantity of food is just sufficient to provide for the growth of the larva to full size, and it pupates in the nest and duly emerges as a winged wasp or bee.

In wasps the ovipositor of the female has become transformed to a sting connected with a poison gland, and the eggs are extruded at the base of it. The solitary wasps hunt insects or spiders to provide subsistence for their larvae, stinging them so as to produce paralysis, but not death, and then storing them in whatever sort of nest the particular species may make. Let us hope they are anaesthetized as well as paralysed, for they are slowly eaten alive by the wasp larvae. If not so treated the prey would be fully active, and liable to injure the delicate newly hatched larva, or else dead, in which case they would quickly putrefy and be unsuitable as food. Each species of wasp chooses a particular kind of prey, some hunt spiders, others caterpillars, or flies, and one infuriates bee keepers by storing honey-bees. The largest solitary wasps are those which hunt the huge Mygalomorph spiders (often inaccurately called tarantulas) of the tropics. Many accounts have been written of the exciting battles between the agile wasp and her huge, formidable adversary, and comparisons are inevitably made with combats between dragons and shining knights with slender swords. Like the knight in the story the wasp always wins.

The solitary bees behave in very much the same way, but, like all bees, feed their young on honey and pollen gathered from flowers. Some of these bees are of great value as pollinators of crops. In the United States at least two species are provided with elaborate artificial premises for breeding, and are cultured in this way in the vicinity of fields of alfalfa. This has led in some areas to a ten-fold increase in production of seed.

The social *Hymenoptera* and their way of life are too familiar to need any introduction. We know more about the Honey-bee than about any other insect. They have been domesticated for a very long time; the Greek historian Herodotus, writing 2,400 years ago, tells how the Egyptian bee keepers put their hives on boats and sailed up the Nile during winter. In the spring they drifted slowly down the river, moving north and

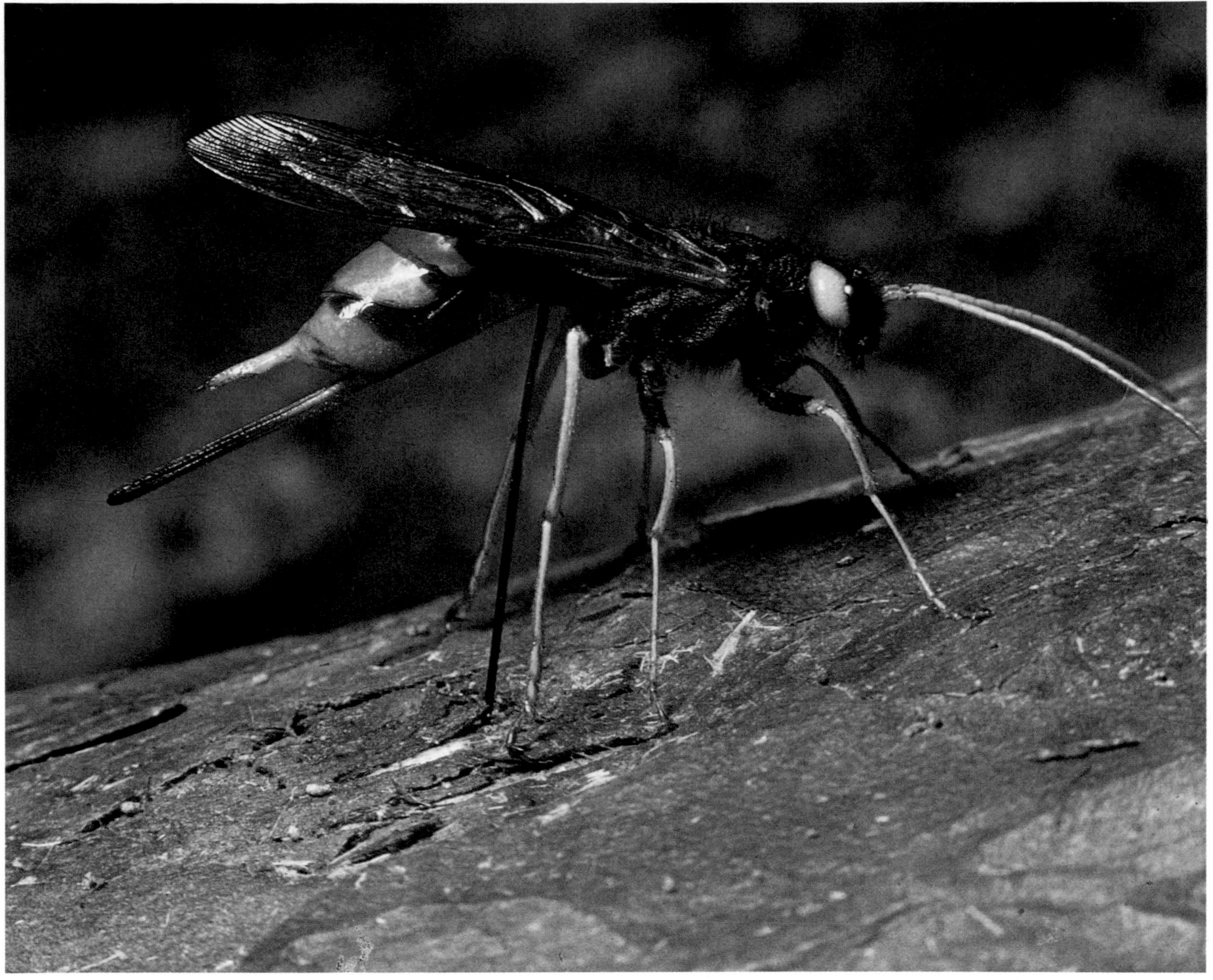

following the spring flush of flowering as it advanced from the south. The population of a hive may number well over 50,000 bees, the vast majority of which are workers, all sterile females, with at least one queen and at certain times other queens and males or drones. In one respect bees, and most other *Hymenoptera* as well, have the advantage of humanity, they can determine the sex of their offspring. A queen bee, soon after hatching, leaves the hive and mates, flying in the air. The sperm she receives is stored in her body and later, when she is mistress of a hive herself, she releases one spermatozoon to fertilize each egg she lays. These eggs produce larvae which all grow into females, workers or queens according to how they are fed. Eggs which are laid without being fertilized produce males, and the queen withholds sperm from some of her eggs when males are needed in the hive. Entire books have been written about the activities and senses and the organization of honey-bees; we cannot devote any more space to it.

A social wasps' nest resembles a honey-bees' in one respect: it contains batteries of hexagonal cells in which eggs are laid and larvae grow and pupate. Nothing could be more different, however, than the materials from which they are made. Bees eat quantities of pollen, rich in protein, and produce from it wax which they excrete, mould with their jaws and use to build their combs. Wasps scrape the surface of dead wood with their jaws and make a pulp with saliva which hardens to form a tough paper. The two groups of insects have evolved quite separately, and we have here a demonstration of how evolution, faced with similar problems against similar backgrounds, arrives at solutions that are closely similar without being identical. Biologists call this convergent evolution.

Rather curiously the ants, though more highly organized than any other social insects, are not master builders or craftsmen – craftswomen perhaps we should say as their workers, like those of the wasps and bees, are all sterile females. Their nests, though enormously populous, show as little sign of planning or design as do our older cities. They do not rear their young in cells, but carry them about from one part of the nest to another, and the nest is usually simply a labyrinth of tunnels and chambers hollowed out of the earth. Ants do the most extraordinary things. They keep other insects as domestic animals and other kinds of ants as slaves. They practise precise and elaborate forms of agriculture and make war on each other. They use their own larvae as instruments for spinning silk. One needs the scope of a whole book to write about ants.

Previous page: left:
Red Ant *(Myrmica ruginodis).* The Red Ant is a common European species that nests under stones and logs in fields, gardens and similar situations. Many kinds of ants live near aphids so that they can feed on the sweet excretions which these insects produce as a result of their living entirely on plant sap, a diet containing a great excess of sugar. By tapping and stroking the aphids with their antennae the ants stimulate them to produce their excretions. Here the ants are shown with black aphids on a plant stem.

Previous page: right:
Giant Wood-wasp *(Urocerus gigas).* In the older books this rather alarming looking insect is called *Sirex gigas.* The spike on the tail of the female is not a sting but an ovipositor and the insect is shown here using this to bore a hole in the bark of a pine tree, into which she will insert an egg. The larva burrows in the wood of pine trees and takes up to three years to mature. It has been introduced in imported timber into Australia and New Zealand and is accounted a serious pest of forests in these countries.

Left:
Ichneumon Wasp *(Ophion luteus).* The Ichneumon wasps are all parasites of other insects, most often of the larvae. The female wasp lays one or more eggs on the intended victim and the larvae from these burrow in its tissues, feeding on them and killing it when they reach maturity. They are of great importance in controlling the numbers of injurious insects. This species is one of the larger Ichneumons and often flies into lighted rooms. It parasitizes the caterpillars of a variety of moths.

Right:
Paper Wasps *(Polistes smithii).* The Polistes wasps are found in most parts of the world in tropical to warm-temperate climates. They represent a rather primitive stage in the evolution of the social wasps. The population of the paper-constructed nests is never so large as in the common social wasps *(Vespula)*, and the queens are hardly distinguishable from the workers apart from their behaviour. This nest was photographed in South Africa and is seen from below. One wasp is chewing a lump of food, the remains of a caterpillar, preparatory to giving it to a larva.

Previous page:
Potter Wasp *(Eumenes).* The Potter Wasps have a wide distribution over the world and are famous for the beautifully shaped urn-like nests which the females make of clay to accommodate their larvae. The larvae are fed on caterpillars, which are stung so that they are paralysed but not killed. In the first of these two photographs of a South African species the wasp is seen laying a single egg in her newly finished nest; in the second she is putting into it a caterpillar, one of the three or four that will provide the wasp larva with enough food to complete its growth. The wasp will make a number of these nests in its lifetime.

Below:
Leaf-cutter Bee *(Megachile).* Many of the solitary bees make nests in burrows or hollow plant stems, which are divided into cells or compartments in each of which is put an egg and a store of honey and pollen to provide food for the larvae. The Leaf-cutter Bees line their nests, and make the partitions, with neatly shaped pieces of living leaves. This bee was photographed in southern England in the act of cutting a circular section of leaf from a rose growing up the side of a house.

Right:
Wool-carder Bee *(Anthidium manicatum).* In this solitary bee the male is much larger and heavier than the female, a state of affairs rather unusual among insects. Its nesting habits are also peculiar, and were noticed by the English naturalist Gilbert White, who wrote about them in the 18th century. The female, shown here at rest on a flower, strips the woolly hair from such plants as mullein and campion and uses it to line her nesting burrow, which is usually one already made and abandoned by some wood-boring insect. Within the lining of plant wool the transparent cells are made and are stocked with honey and pollen for the larvae to feed on.

Left:
Bumble-bee *(Bombus lucorum).* The Bumble-bees are among the most familiar insects of temperate regions and are unusual among insect groups in being more abundant and varied in cool climates than in the tropics. They are social bees but show a far lower degree of organization than the Honey-bees, and the workers in a nest seldom exceed three or four hundred in number. This species nests underground, usually in an abandoned mouse hole. Bumble-bees are valuable as pollinators of various plants, especially clover, and until they were introduced from Europe to New Zealand this crop would never set seed satisfactorily there.

Below:
Desert Ants *(Camponotus detritus).* The ants shown fighting each other in this picture are inhabitants of the Namib Desert in south-western Africa. This is one of the most ancient deserts in the world and many of the insects found there have special adaptations for coping with the heat and lack of water. Ants are pugnacious insects and will fight readily with other species of ants and even with individuals of their own species if they come from another colony or nest.

Right:
Cocktail Ants *(Crematogaster).* These ants have got their name from the habit of raising their abdomen up over their back when they get agitated, so that its tip points forward. At the same time they expose a white gland at the tip of the tail which gives off an unpleasant smell. They also bite viciously. This is a South African species and workers are shown in the nest attending the pupae; an adult winged ant is also in the picture. The pupae are white with dark eyes and have the legs and antennae free from the body. In this group of ants, the *Myrmicinae*, they are not enclosed in cocoons.

Camouflage and Warning Colours

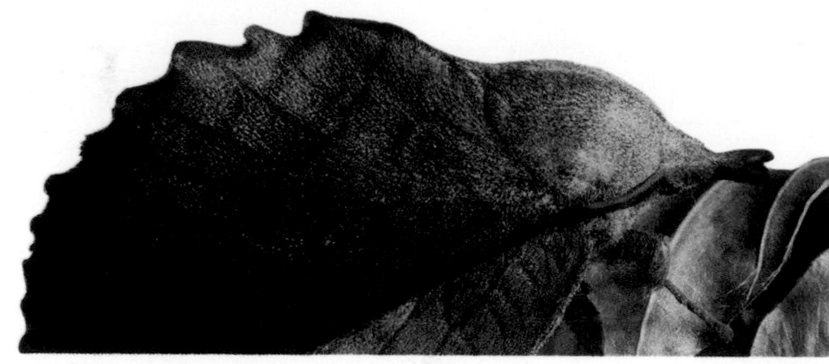

Examples of natural camouflage are more numerous and varied among insects than any other group of animals. This is largely, of course, because insects themselves are so very numerous and diverse, but there are other reasons. The enemies that hunt them by sight, mainly birds, are much larger than they are, so that most insects are defenceless against them. Their small size makes them easy to conceal; it is easier to hide a thimble than a top hat. Finally the birds have keener eyesight than any other animals, so that a high degree of perfection is required in devices for hiding from them.

The first principle of camouflage is to be coloured like your background. If you take an umbrella and hold it upside-down under the leafy branch of a tree and shake the branch, a number of insects will fall into it, caterpillars, small bugs, beetles, bush-crickets and many other kinds, and a large proportion of them will be green. This colour, without any additional adaptation, makes insects difficult to see among leaves. Insects collected from leaf litter on the woodland floor will be predominantly brown, few or none of them green.

The next step towards perfection in natural camouflage is the development of what are called disruptive patterns to break up the outline of the animal and conceal its shape. This is more important in larger animals, but is often seen in insects which sit in the open on tree trunks and branches. A bold dark and light pattern, combined with resemblance to the background, will give more effective concealment than an even tone all over. Grasshoppers are often striped dark and pale green which makes them hard to see when they are sitting on grass stems.

This brings us to the most refined level of camouflage, the actual simulation of definite items in the environment, and it is here that insects excel far beyond most other animals. Objects to be copied must be inedible, or at any rate not sought out as food by birds or other animals. Leaves, green and alive or withered and brown, are often simulated by butterflies and moths, whose broad coloured wings afford ideal material for natural selection to work upon. Many butterflies have an outline, when sitting with closed wings, that closely resembles a leaf, and in some cases the colour and pattern completes the resemblance with extraordinary perfection, as in the famous Indian Leaf butterfly. Some kinds of mantis are shaped and coloured so like flowers that they actually lure insects which habitually seek out flowers for nectar and pollen and seize them when they approach. Here the deception serves two purposes, for it also gives the mantis protection against being seen by birds.

A number of moths have a pattern on the wings remarkably like that of moss or lichen growing on a tree trunk, so that they virtually disappear when at rest on this type of background. Another curious trick of simulation practised by small moths, and also by the young caterpillars of swallowtail butterflies, is to imitate the droppings of birds. These little black-and-white deposits are very frequently seen adhering to leaves; the insects that imitate them habitually sit on leaves and hungry birds naturally pass them by.

The behaviour of the insect usually plays an important part in making its concealing colour and pattern effective. Obviously it must choose a suitable background on which to rest, and when at rest it must keep perfectly still. A grasshopper among herbage is difficult to find, but if it hops the sharp eyes of a bird will mark where it comes to rest again. In the tropics white herons or egrets may often be seen following grazing cattle and buffaloes. The trampling of the beasts disturbs the insects in the grass, and any grasshopper that panics and jumps is instantly seized by one of the egrets.

Many caterpillars are coloured and patterned to resemble twigs. The effect of this is greatly enhanced by their habit of resting by holding on with the hindmost legs and holding the body out stiff and straight, so that the insect appears like one twig growing out of another. The tropical and sub-tropical stick-insects have the body and legs so elongate and thin that no explanation of their name is needed. Many of them improve on the resemblance to sticks by adopting curious attitudes by which they not only look like sticks but wholly cease to look like insects. Some moths which simulate pieces of broken twig will drop to the ground if disturbed and lie motionless, still well concealed on the litter of a woodland floor.

A number of insects are noticeable by the fact that their colours seem designed to make them conspicuous against the background of their habitats. Many of them are boldly marked with black and yellow or black and red. Smelling or tasting these insects will often reveal an unpleasant odour or flavour, and some of them, such as wasps, are armed with venomous stings. Young birds do not have an instinctive fear or dislike of these insects, but one or two trials, in which the insect may be fatally injured, are enough to teach the bird that these are creatures best left alone. The more conspicuously coloured the insect is the more readily will the birds learn their lesson, and for the sacrifice of a few of their number the rest gain a valuable degree of immunity from attack.

Among the commonest of insects protected in this way are some of the bugs of the *Heteroptera* group, which are often black with startling red, yellow or white patterns. To our eyes they appear striking or even beautiful, but their colours have no relevance to giving us pleasure; they are warnings like the equally boldly coloured signs that are put up to warn motorists of dangerous hazards on the road.

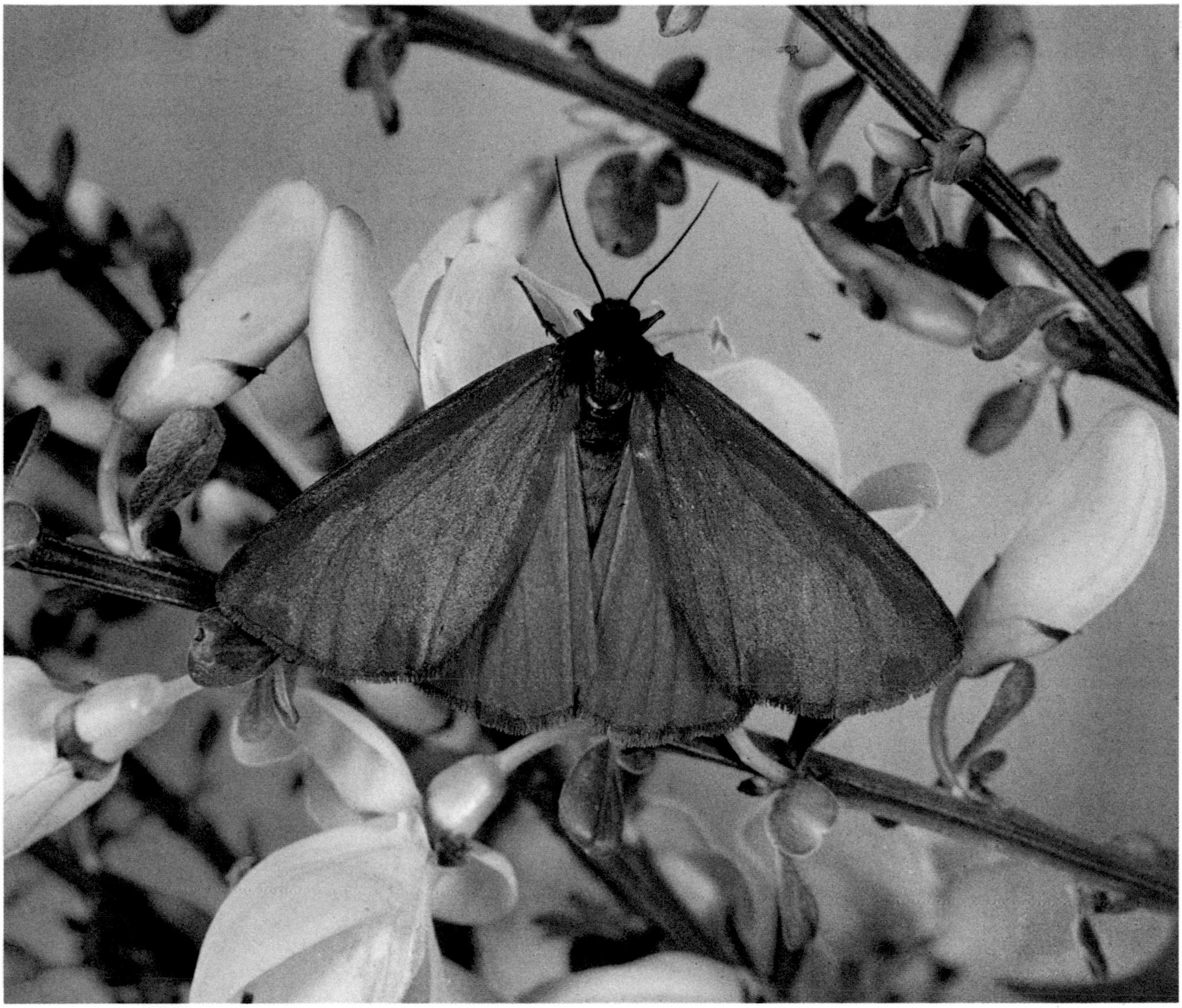

Many butterflies and moths gain protection in this way and some of them obtain the poisonous substances in their bodies from the plants on which they fed as larvae. This is true of the family of butterflies called *Danaidae*, of which the well-known American Monarch is a member. The Monarch caterpillar feeds on species of Asclepias or milkweeds, and has the ability to accept their poisonous sap into its system without ill effect, and also to store it so that it is still present in the body of the pupa and the butterfly. It is not ill tasting but has the effect on birds of making them vomit violently and painfully very soon after their ill-chosen meal, and they associate their meal with the discomfort which they have suffered. The well-known day-flying moths called Burnets, which are found all over Europe and western Asia, are intensely distasteful to birds. If a bird inadvertently takes a burnet it immediately lets go of it and wipes its beak, salivating copiously. Almost all the burnets are luridly coloured, with red the dominant element in the pattern.

In parts of America where the Monarch butterfly is found there is another quite unrelated species, the Viceroy (*Limenitis archippus*) which closely resembles the Monarch in colour and pattern. It is quite edible, and if aviary birds, with no experience of butterflies in the wild, are given Viceroys, they will eat them without hesitation. If, however, they are given Monarchs they soon learn that these are unwholesome, and then they will not touch Viceroys either. These experiments suggest that the mimicry of the Monarch by the Viceroy is probably effective in the wild in giving the latter protection against attack by birds.

Protective mimicry of this kind is very widespread among insects. Many of them, hover-flies, beetles and some moths have evolved so as to resemble wasps, which are both ill tasting and armed with a sting. The big Drone-fly (*Eristalis tenax*) is so like a bee that very few people will take one in their fingers if it is buzzing on a window pane. Among some tropical butterflies mimicry associations become so complex that we can only allude to them without attempting to describe them in any great detail.

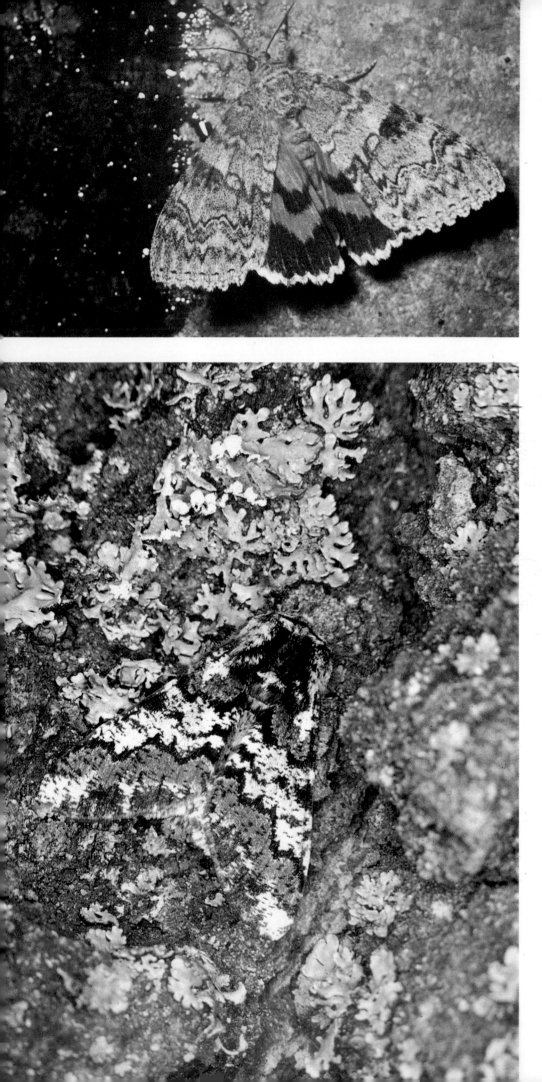

Previous page: left:
Lappet Moth *(Gastropacha quercifolia).* This rather large European moth can look just like a pile of dead and withered leaves. Not only are the colours and pattern of its wings well adapted for this camouflage, but its attitude at rest greatly enhances the effect. The hind-wings are pushed forward so that their rounded margins appear in front of the fore-wings, breaking up the outline of the insect and producing an appearance of overlapping leaves.

Previous page: right:
Cinnabar Moth *(Callimorpha jacobaeae).* This pretty black and bright pink moth provides an excellent example of warning coloration. The insect is conspicuous because it gains advantage from being readily recognized as inedible by birds which have already tasted and rejected one or two of the moths. The food plant of the larva is Ragwort and the moth retains poisonous alkaloids from the plant, as well as itself secreting histamine. The larva is also inedible and has a conspicuous pattern of orange and black rings all along the body.

Top left:
Red Underwing Moth *(Catocala nupta).* When this handsome moth is at rest during the day the red-and-black hind-wings are concealed by the mottled grey fore-wings, which simulate the bark of a tree trunk. If the insect is closely approached or touched, it will fly off, producing a sudden explosion of bright colour, and when it settles again it disappears in an almost magical way. This so-called 'flash coloration' has the effect of startling a predator that disturbs the insect and of puzzling a pursuer when the moth comes to rest.

Below left:
Oak Beauty Moth *(Biston strataria).* Woodland moths that fly early in the year, when the trees are still bare of leaves, are often well camouflaged against a background of moss- and lichen-covered bark. The Oak Beauty emerges from the pupa in March and rests by day on the trunks and branches of trees in the oak woods in which its larva feeds. This is a common species over most of Britain and Europe.

Top right:
Buff-tip Moth *(Phalera bucephala).* When at rest this moth wraps its wings round its body so that it has a cylindrical shape, and its coloration makes it look remarkably like a broken piece of twig. The buff-coloured wing-tips represent the bare wood exposed where the twig has snapped at one end, the yellow-brown thorax the other broken end, and the intervening part of the wings is greyish-brown like smooth bark. It is a common British and European species.

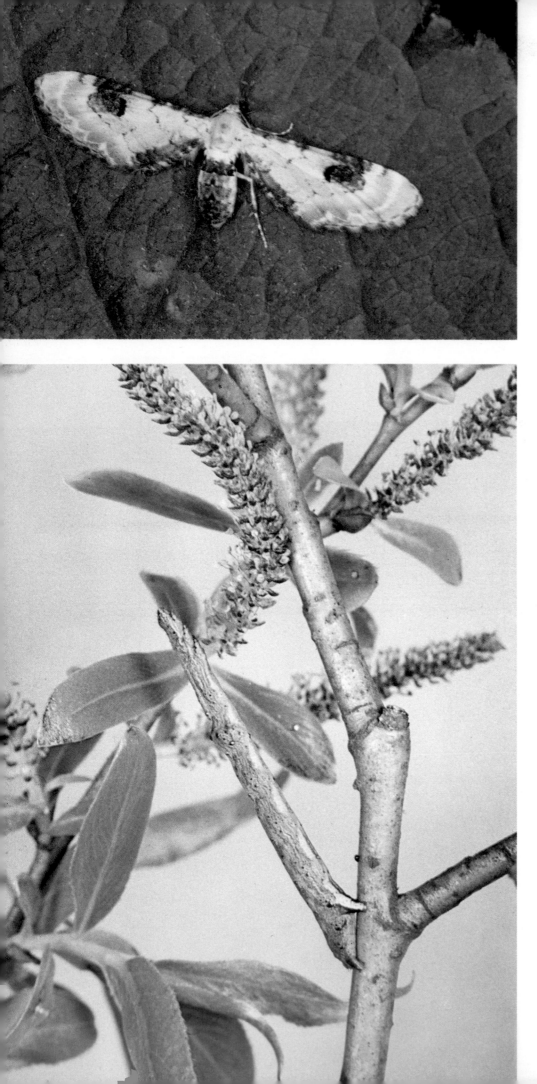

Previous page: below right:
Rock Grayling Butterfly *(Hipparchia alcyone).* The Grayling butterflies are inhabitants of downs, heaths and open woodland and frequently settle on the ground. The colour and pattern of the underside of their wings is well adapted for concealment against a background of exposed soil, stones and vegetable debris, and the irregular pale band on the hind-wing provides a disruptive pattern which breaks up the butterfly's outline. The Rock Grayling is a common species of central and southern Europe and western Asia. This one was photographed in Spain.

Left:
Lime-speck Pug Moth *(Eupithecia centaureata).* In bushes and hedgerows one never need search for long for leaves splashed with the characteristic white and blackish droppings of birds. The ever-resourceful insects have, in the course of their evolution, taken advantage of the abundance of these droppings by imitating their appearance. Quite a number of small moths which spend the day sitting motionless on leaves have a colour and pattern that obviously simulates bird droppings. It would be hard to imagine a more effective disguise for protection against insectivorous birds.

Below left:
Bordered Beauty Moth *(Epione repandaria).* This is the larva of the pretty Geometrid moth whose picture appears on page 44. We have here a most perfect example of how well-camouflaged creatures can be, particularly when their shape and colour is combined with appropriate behaviour to produce the camouflage effect. When it is not feeding, the caterpillar holds onto a twig with its two pairs of hinder legs and keeps its body rigidly extended at an angle consistent with that of one twig growing out of another. The three pairs of legs just behind the head are laid forwards and hardly break the outline of this beautifully adapted 'living stick'.

Right:
Ground-hopper (Family *Pamphagidae*). The ground-hoppers are allied to the grasshoppers and locusts and adapted for life on the ground. This South African species has its habitat in dry, stony places and has evolved an extraordinarily perfect resemblance to a stone. It is seen in dorsal view, and every visible part of the body takes part in the simulation. Even the eyes and antennae are stone coloured. The dorsal shield of the thorax is rugged and has rounded angles and the legs are rounded and thickened.

Left:
Common Wasp *(Vespula vulgaris).* Yellow and black, red and black, these are the most usual colour combinations evolved by insects to give warning that they are unpleasant to eat or dangerous. Rather unexpectedly, common wasps are both. Mashed up wasps, fed to birds, are tasted and rejected with the usual signs of disgust. Also, of course, wasps have formidable stings, and it is not surprising that they have developed an unmistakable warning pattern. This and the very similar German Wasp *(Vespula germanica)* are the two species which are a nuisance in late summer, when their paper nests are at their most populous.

Below left:
Wasp Beetle *(Clytus arietis).* This is a harmless and probably quite tasty beetle that has developed a wasp-like yellow and black uniform, which probably gives it some degree of protection from birds. Its quick, jerky movements and habit of running about on leaves and flowers make it look even more like a wasp, and this is clearly a case of protective mimicry, similar to that of the hover-flies mentioned on page 46. It is one of the longhorn beetles *(Cerambycidae)* and its larvae burrow in the dead wood of posts and fallen trees. It is common in Europe and southern England in June and July.

Bottom left:
Provence Burnet Moth *(Zygaena occitanica).* To our eyes the brilliant colours of this southern European moth give it an attractive and beautiful appearance, but its vivid coloration was certainly not evolved to give pleasure to any beholder. All the Burnet moths have intensely distasteful and poisonous body fluids, which include hydrogen cyanide and histamine in their composition. Any young and inexperienced bird that pecks at a Burnet moth will reject it with obvious disgust and will afterwards avoid attacking any insect that it recognizes as a Burnet. Conspicuous colours are easily recognized and therefore serve to protect the insect by giving warning that it is inedible.

Right:
Grasshopper *(Maura regulosa).* A variety of grasshopper species is protected by being ill-tasting and poisonous, and most of them improve the effect by discharging poisonous fluid in the form of a bubbly froth from openings in the side of the body. This South African species advertises its unpleasantness by means of a red-and-black uniform. This colour combination seems to be very effective in conveying the appropriate message to birds and is encountered in a wide variety of distasteful insects, including the Burnet and Cinnabar moths, the Ladybirds among the beetles, and grasshoppers, as in the present instance.

Acknowledgements

The publishers would like to thank the following organizations for their kind permission to reproduce the pictures in this book:

F G H Allen	39.
F Baillie Natural History Photographic Agency	31, 72.
Anthony Bannister N H P A	endpapers, 2-3, 9, 11 bottom, 13, 17, 18 top & bottom, 19, 23 top, 25, 26 top, 29 bottom, 48-9, 50 top, 57, 58, 59, 62 bottom, 63, 69, 71.
N A Callow N H P A	14 top, 70 top.
James A Cox Washington	11 top, 15, 16, 23 bottom, 41, 42 bottom, 43.
Stephen Dalton N H P A	1, 4, 6 bottom, 7, 8, 10 bottom, 27 top, 29 top, 38 bottom, 42 top, 50 bottom, 62 top.
Michael Davies N H P A	30.
Eric Elms N H P A	34 top, 35, 40 top.
D P Healey N H P A	10 top, 24 bottom, 55.
A B Klots	37 top, 40 centre.
J L Mason N H P A	5, 36 top.
L Hugh Newman F R E S N H P A	33, 36 bottom, 38 top, 45 bottom.
G Temple N H P A	64.
M W F Tweedie N H P A	6 top, 12, 14 bottom, 18 centre, 20, 21, 22, 24, 26 bottom, 27 bottom, 28, 29 bottom, 32, 34 bottom, 37 bottom, 40 bottom, 42 left, 44, 45 top, 46, 47, 51, 52, 53, 54, 56, 60, 61, 65, 66, 67, 68, 70 centre & bottom.

Endpapers:
Potato Ladybirds *(Epilachna dregei).* Although most ladybirds are predators on plant lice, one subfamily of them, the *Epilachninae*, are vegetable feeders, and this species lives on potato plants. Ladybirds in general are protected from birds and other animals by having an unpleasant taste and smell. Almost all of them hibernate during the winter, massed together in thousands, and in this way they make their odour perceptible and discourage enemies from attacking them. A solitary ladybird might very well be pecked or bitten before its enemy realized that it was inedible.